Contents

428·4
IELTS/
UCL

Official IELTS Practice Materials
(formerly IELTS Specimen Materials 2003)

There is also a CD containing the Listening test and three candidate Speaking tests.

Introduction

These Practice Materials should be read in conjunction with *IELTS Information for candidates*.

The main purpose of the Practice Materials is to give IELTS candidates an idea of what the test is like. They also give candidates the opportunity to test themselves to see whether their English is at the level required.

In the past some people who took the test did not reach the standard of English needed to be accepted at the institution of their choice. They spent time and money taking a test which was far too difficult for them. We hope that using the Practice Materials will stop this happening. People who intend to take the test can complete the question papers in this booklet, mark them themselves and see whether their scores are good enough for them to attempt the test itself. A high score on these practice papers, however, does not guarantee that the same standard will be reached in the real test.

These Practice Materials are approved by British Council, Cambridge ESOL and IDP: IELTS Australia.

Format of the IELTS Test

An IELTS test is made up of four sub-tests. All candidates take the same Listening and Speaking tests. There is a choice of Reading and Writing tests depending on whether you are an **ACADEMIC** or **GENERAL TRAINING** candidate.

The tests are normally taken in the order Listening, Reading, Writing, Speaking, and are timed as follows:

Listening	approximately 30 minutes
Reading	60 minutes
Writing	60 minutes
Speaking	11–14 minutes

Information on the test format can be found in *IELTS Information for candidates*. This is available from test centres or can be downloaded from the IELTS website **www.ielts.org**

The website also contains further information on the test content, test administration and marking procedures.

This Practice Materials booklet contains complete samples of the Listening, Reading, Writing and Speaking tests.

How to take the Practice Test

If you are planning to take the Practice Test you should follow these steps.

1. Decide which of the Reading and Writing tests you should take – **ACADEMIC** or **GENERAL TRAINING**.

   The **ACADEMIC** module assesses the English language skills required for academic study or professional recognition.

   The emphasis of the **GENERAL TRAINING** module is on basic survival skills in a broad social and educational context. It is suitable for candidates who are going to English-speaking countries to complete their secondary education, to undertake work experience or training programmes not at degree level, or for immigration purposes to Australia, Canada and New Zealand.

2. You need to write on or photocopy the answer sheets. These are the sheets where you will write your answers. The Listening/Reading answer sheets are on pages 79–80. Instructions on how to complete the answer sheets can be found on page 78. The Writing answer sheets are on pages 81–84.

3. Prepare for the Practice Test carefully:

   (a) Find a quiet room with a table to write on.

   (b) Make sure that you are not going to be interrupted.

   (c) Make sure that you have everything you need, i.e. pencils, pens, an eraser, a pencil sharpener and a CD player for the Listening test.

   (d) Make sure you have a watch or clock. It is essential that you follow the time allowed for each paper. There is a lot of material in the Reading and Writing tests and one of the aims of this Practice Test is to see how you can manage in the time allowed. **If you allow yourself longer than the test says, you will not get a true picture of your ability.**

4. Turn to the Listening test on page 1. Do not open it yet. Put the Listening CD in the CD player. Do not play it yet.

5. Read the instructions on the cover of the question paper and make sure you understand them. Once you are sure you do, start the Listening CD. Note that once you have started it, you must not stop it. You must let it run straight through to the end. It will take about 30 minutes. You should write your answers in the spaces provided next to the questions on the question paper. Write your answers as you listen.

   When you take the real test at a test centre, you will be asked to copy your answers onto the answer sheet (on page 79). You will be given 10 minutes to do this after the end of the test.

6. Once the recording has ended, do not listen to it again.

7. Now turn to the appropriate Reading test (**ACADEMIC** or **GENERAL TRAINING**) on pages 10 or 32. Do not open the question paper yet. Read the instructions on the cover of the question paper. Once you are sure you understand them, make a note of the time. Start the test.

8. Open the Reading question paper. Remember to answer all the questions by writing the appropriate answers in the corresponding box numbers on the answer sheet on page 80. For example, write the answer to question 1 in box 1.

9. After 60 minutes, stop **immediately**. This will give you a good idea of how you would have managed the Reading test under examination conditions. Please note that no extra time is allowed to transfer the answers to the answer sheet.

10. Allow yourself a short break.

11. Now turn to the appropriate Writing test (**ACADEMIC** or **GENERAL TRAINING**). There are three examples of Academic Writing on pages 23–31. There are two examples of General Training Writing on pages 44–49. Write your answers on the Writing Answer Sheets (pages 81–84).

12. After 60 minutes stop **immediately**. This will give you a good idea of how you would have managed the Writing test under examination conditions.

13. Read 'How to mark the Listening and Reading Practice Tests' on page 52, and then check your answers to the Listening and Reading tests against those in the answer keys on pages 53–61. Put a tick beside each correct answer and a cross beside each wrong one. Each tick is worth one mark. Sometimes more than one piece of information is needed for one mark. Make sure you follow the instructions in the answer keys carefully.

14. Check your marks again to make sure you have not made any mistakes.

15. Add up the ticks and write down the totals for the Listening and Reading tests. Do this twice to make sure you have not made any mistakes.

16. You should now have one score for Listening and another for Reading. Check your scores against the comments which precede each of the answer keys.

17. You cannot mark the Writing test yourself but you will have a clearer idea of what is required in the time allowed. There is information on how Writing is assessed on page 62.

18. You will find sample answers to the Writing tasks on pages 63–75. Each answer has been marked and given a Band Score with examiner comments.

19. You will find three sample Speaking tests on the CD. There is information on how Speaking is assessed on page 76. On page 77 there are Band Scores and examiner comments on these candidate performances.

Re-using the Practice Materials

If your scores on the Practice Test are low and you decide to have more English lessons or study to improve a language skill, you may want to take the test again to see if you have made progress before you apply to take IELTS. You should, therefore, put the Practice Materials away and not refer to them until you are ready to try again. If you do this, there is a good chance that you will have forgotten the answers and that the Practice Materials will still give you a reasonable indication of the score you would get on IELTS. You should therefore not re-take the Practice Test too soon after first taking it.

Please note that the Practice Materials are not designed to measure short-term progress. If you re-take the test too soon, you may find that your scores are no higher than they were.

INTERNATIONAL ENGLISH LANGUAGE TESTING SYSTEM

LISTENING

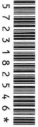

PRACTICE MATERIALS   Approx. 30 minutes

TIME   Approx. 30 minutes

INSTRUCTIONS TO CANDIDATES

Do not open this question booklet until you are told to do so.

Write your name and candidate number in the spaces at the top of this page.

Answer **all** questions.

Write your answers in the question booklet **as you listen**. At the end of the test, you will be given **ten minutes** to transfer your answers to the **separate answer sheet**.

Do not remove this booklet from the examination room.

INFORMATION FOR CANDIDATES

There are **40** questions in this question booklet. All questions carry one mark.

The test is divided into four sections.

You will hear each section **ONCE** only.

There will be pauses to allow you to look at the questions and a 30-second pause at the end of each section to review your answers.

SECTION 1   Questions 1 – 10

Questions 1 and 2

Label the map below.

*Write the correct letter, **A-H**, next to questions 1 and 2.*

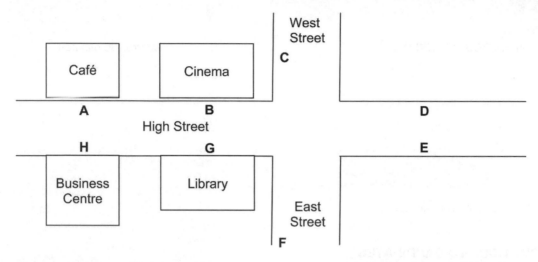

Example	
Mrs Reynolds:	*B*

1   Elderly woman: ....

2   Thieves' car: ....

Questions 3 – 5

*Choose the correct letter, **A**, **B** or **C**.*

3   When Mrs Reynolds saw the thieves, she

        A   ran after them.
        B   telephoned the police.
        C   went to help the elderly woman.

4   The elderly woman was

        A   badly hurt.
        B   unhurt.
        C   very upset.

5   Which woman had once had her bag stolen in the past?

        A   the elderly woman
        B   Mrs Reynolds
        C   Mrs Reynolds' friend

Question 6

*Choose **TWO** letters, **A-F**.*

6   The bag contained

        A   a purse.
        B   £50.
        C   a cheque book.
        D   a cheque card.
        E   a bus pass.
        F   a door key.

Questions 7 – 10

Complete the table below.

*Write **NO MORE THAN TWO WORDS AND/OR A NUMBER** for each answer.*

	age	build	hair colour	distinguishing marks
younger man	about 17	**7**	**8**	none
older man	about **9**	medium	brown	a **10** .... on chin

SECTION 2   *Questions 11 – 20*

Questions 11 – 13

*Choose the correct letter, **A**, **B** or **C**.*

11   The Bridge Hotel is located in

        A   the city centre.
        B   the country.
        C   the suburbs.

12   The newest sports facility in the hotel is

        A   a swimming pool.
        B   a fitness centre.
        C   a tennis court.

13   The hotel restaurant specialises in

        A   healthy food.
        B   local food.
        C   international food.

Questions 14 and 15

*Choose **TWO** letters, **A-E**.*

Which **TWO** business facilities are mentioned?

        A   internet access
        B   mobile phone hire
        C   audio-visual facilities
        D   airport transport
        E   translation services

Questions 16 – 20

Complete the table below.

Write **NO MORE THAN THREE WORDS AND/OR A NUMBER** *for each answer.*

Short Break Packages		
Length of stay	**Cost (per person per night)**	**Special features**
2 days	**16** £	Full cooked breakfast Entertainment in the **17** ....
3 days	£60	As above, plus: – a **18** ....
5 days	**19** £	As above, plus: – 2 days' free beauty therapy – full-day membership of a **20** ....

SECTION 3   *Questions 21 – 30*

Questions 21 and 22

Complete the sentences below.

Write **NO MORE THAN TWO WORDS AND/OR A NUMBER** *for each answer.*

21   Last year, Dina got a grade .... for the Theory and Practice option.

22   Dina has some free time because her .... has been cancelled.

Question 23

Choose **ONE** *letter,* **A-E***.*

Which book does Dina advise against?

       A   Brown: Observing Theory in Practice
       B   Jespersen: Theory's Crucible
       C   Piresi: On Giants' Shoulders
       D   Willard: Practical Theories in the Social Sciences
       E   Williams: Knowledge Theory

Questions 24 – 30

Complete the notes below.

*Write **NO MORE THAN TWO WORDS AND/OR A NUMBER** for each answer.*

How to use the Recall System

Take a **24** .... from librarian's desk.

Complete the details of the book. Write your **25** .... address on back. Hand it in at the **26** ....

Check mail in your department twice a day to see if book is ready to collect. It normally takes 3 days.

Cost: **27** .... per book.

Dina's advice on organising a study group to work on an assignment

Find two or three people on the course who live near you.

Divide up the reading load.

Take it in turns to **28** .... what you have read for the others.

Explain your **29** .... to each other.

Write first draft of essay.

Exchange drafts and **30** ....

Write final version of essay.

SECTION 4   Questions 31 – 40

Questions 31 – 33

Complete the sentences below.

*Write **NO MORE THAN THREE WORDS** for each answer.*

Peregrine Falcons

31   The Peregrine falcons found in .... are not migratory birds.

32   There is disagreement about their maximum ....

33   When the female is guarding the nest, the male spends most of his time ....

Questions 34 – 37

Complete the table below.

*Write **NO MORE THAN THREE WORDS** for each answer.*

Age of falcons	What occurs
20 days old	The falcons **34** ....
28 days old	The falcons are **35** ....
2 months old	The falcons **36** .... permanently
1-12 months old	More than half of falcons **37** ....

Questions 38 – 40

Complete the notes below.

*Write **NO MORE THAN THREE WORDS** for each answer.*

Procedures used for field research on Peregrine falcon chicks

First:	catch chicks
Second:	**38** .... to legs
Third:	**39** .... of chicks
Fourth:	take blood sample to assess level of pesticide
Fifth:	check the **40** .... of the birds

INTERNATIONAL ENGLISH LANGUAGE TESTING SYSTEM

ACADEMIC READING

PRACTICE MATERIALS

1 hour

TIME   1 hour

INSTRUCTIONS TO CANDIDATES

Do not open this question booklet until you are told to do so.

Write your name and candidate number in the spaces at the top of this page.

Answer **all** questions.

Write your answers on the **separate answer sheet**. If you write your answers in the question booklet, you must copy them onto the separate answer sheet **within the time limit**.

Do not remove this booklet from the examination room.

INFORMATION FOR CANDIDATES

There are **40** questions in this question booklet. All questions carry one mark.

The test is divided into three sections.

*You should spend about 20 minutes on **Questions 1-14**, which are based on Reading Passage 1.*

Spider silk cuts weight of bridges

A strong, light bio-material made by genes from spiders could transform construction and industry

A   Scientists have succeeded in copying the silk-producing genes of the *Golden Orb Weaver* spider and are using them to create a synthetic material which they believe is the model for a new generation of advanced bio-materials. The new material, biosilk, which has been spun for the first time by researchers at DuPont, has an enormous range of potential uses in construction and manufacturing.

B   The attraction of the silk spun by the spider is a combination of great strength and enormous elasticity, which man-made fibres have been unable to replicate. On an equal-weight basis, spider silk is far stronger than steel and it is estimated that if a single strand could be made about 10m in diameter, it would be strong enough to stop a jumbo jet in flight. A third important factor is that it is extremely light. Army scientists are already looking at the possibilities of using it for lightweight, bullet-proof vests and parachutes.

C   For some time, biochemists have been trying to synthesise the drag-line silk of the *Golden Orb Weaver*. The drag-line silk, which forms the radial arms of the web, is stronger than the other parts of the web and some biochemists believe a synthetic version could prove to be as important a material as nylon, which has been around for 50 years, since the discoveries of Wallace Carothers and his team ushered in the age of polymers.

D   To recreate the material, scientists, including Randolph Lewis at the University of Wyoming, first examined the silk-producing gland of the spider. 'We took out the glands that produce the silk and looked at the coding for the protein material they make, which is spun into a web. We then went looking for clones with the right DNA,' he says.

E   At DuPont, researchers have used both yeast and bacteria as hosts to grow the raw material, which they have spun into fibres. Robert Dorsch, DuPont's director of biochemical development, says the globules of protein, comparable with marbles in an egg, are harvested and processed. 'We break open the bacteria, separate out the globules of protein and use them as the raw starting material. With yeast, the gene system can be designed so that the material excretes the protein outside the yeast for better access,' he says.

F   'The bacteria and the yeast produce the same protein, equivalent to that which the spider uses in the drag lines of the web. The spider mixes the protein into a water-based solution and then spins it into a solid fibre in one go. Since we are not as clever as the spider and we are not using such sophisticated organisms, we substituted man-made approaches and dissolved the protein in chemical solvents, which are then spun to push the material through small holes to form the solid fibre.'

G   Researchers at DuPont say they envisage many possible uses for a new biosilk material. They say that earthquake-resistant suspension bridges hung from cables of synthetic spider silk fibres may become a reality. Stronger ropes, safer seat belts, shoe soles that do not wear out so quickly and tough new clothing are among the other applications. Biochemists such as Lewis see the potential range of uses of biosilk as almost limitless. 'It is very strong and retains elasticity; there are no man-made materials that can mimic both these properties. It is also a biological material with all the advantages that has over petrochemicals,' he says.

H   At DuPont's laboratories, Dorsch is excited by the prospect of new super-strong materials but he warns they are many years away. 'We are at an early stage but theoretical predictions are that we will wind up with a very strong, tough material, with an ability to absorb shock, which is stronger and tougher than the man-made materials that are conventionally available to us,' he says.

I   The spider is not the only creature that has aroused the interest of material scientists. They have also become envious of the natural adhesive secreted by the sea mussel. It produces a protein adhesive to attach itself to rocks. It is tedious and expensive to extract the protein from the mussel, so researchers have already produced a synthetic gene for use in surrogate bacteria.

Questions 1 – 5

Reading Passage 1 has nine paragraphs, **A-I**.

Which paragraph contains the following information?

*Write the correct letter, **A-I**, in boxes 1-5 on your answer sheet.*

1   a comparison of the ways two materials are used to replace silk-producing glands

2   predictions regarding the availability of the synthetic silk

3   ongoing research into other synthetic materials

4   the research into the part of the spider that manufactures silk

5   the possible application of the silk in civil engineering

Questions 6 – 11

Complete the flow-chart below.

*Choose **NO MORE THAN THREE WORDS** from the passage for each answer.*

Write your answers in boxes 6-11 on your answer sheet.

Synthetic gene grown in **6** .... or **7** ....

⬇

globules of **8** ....

⬇

dissolved in **9** ....

⬇

passed through **10** ....

⬇

to produce **11** ....

Questions 12 – 14

Do the following statements agree with the information given in Reading Passage 1?

In boxes 12-14 on your answer sheet, write

TRUE	*if the statement agrees with the information*
FALSE	*if the statement contradicts the information*
NOT GIVEN	*if there is no information on this*

12   Biosilk has already replaced nylon in parachute manufacture.

13   The spider produces silk of varying strengths.

14   Lewis and Dorsch co-operated in the synthetic production of silk.

READING PASSAGE 2

*You should spend about 20 minutes on **Questions 15-27**, which are based on Reading Passage 2.*

TEACHING IN UNIVERSITIES

In the 19th century, an American academic, Newman, characterised a university as:

'a place of teaching universal knowledge...(a place for) the diffusion
and extension of knowledge rather than its advancement.'

Newman argued that if universities were not for teaching but rather for scientific discovery, then they would not need students.

Interestingly, during the 20th century, while still teaching thousands of students each year, the resources of most universities have been steadily channelled away from teaching into research activities. Most recently, however, there have been strong moves in both North America and the United Kingdom to develop initiatives that would enhance the profile of the teaching institutions of higher education. In the near future, therefore, as well as the intrinsic rewards gained from working with students and the sense that they are contributing to their overall growth and development, there should soon be extrinsic rewards, in the form of job promotion, for those pursuing academic excellence in teaching in universities.

In the future, there will be more focus in universities on the quality of their graduates and their progression rates. Current degree courses, whose assessment strategies require students to learn by rote and reiterate the course material, and which do not require the student to interact with the material, or construct a personal meaning about it or even to understand the discipline, are resulting in poor learning outcomes. This traditional teaching approach does not take into account modern theories of education, the individual needs of the learner, nor his or her prior learning experience.

In order for universities to raise both the quality and status of teaching, it is first necessary to have some kind of understanding of what constitutes good practice. A 1995 report, compiled in Australia, lists eight qualities that researchers agree are essential to good teaching.

Good teachers...

A   are themselves good learners – resulting in teaching that is dynamic, reflective and constantly evolving as they learn more and more about teaching;

B   display enthusiasm for their subject and the desire to share it with their students;

C   recognise the importance of context and adjust their teaching accordingly;

D   encourage deep learning approaches and are concerned with developing their students' critical thinking skills, problem-solving skills and problem-approach behaviours;

E   demonstrate an ability to transform and extend knowledge, rather than merely transmit it;

F   recognise individual differences in their students and take advantage of these;

G   set clear goals, use valid assessment techniques and provide high-quality feedback to their students;

H   show respect for, and interest in, their students and sustain high expectations of them.

In addition to aiming to engage students in the learning process, there is also a need to address the changing needs of the marketplace. Because in many academic disciplines the body of relevant knowledge is growing at an exponential rate, it is no longer possible, or even desirable, for an individual to have a complete knowledge base. Rather, it is preferable that he or she should have an understanding of the concepts and the principles of the subject, have the ability to apply this understanding to new situations and have the wherewithal to seek out the information that is needed.

As the world continues to increase in complexity, university graduates will need to be equipped to cope with rapid changes in technology and to enter careers that may not yet be envisaged, with change of profession being commonplace. To produce graduates equipped for this workforce, it is essential that educators teach in ways that encourage learners to engage in deep learning which may be built upon in the later years of their course, and also be transferred to the workplace.

The new role of the university teacher, then, is one that focuses on the students' learning rather than the instructor's teaching. The syllabus is more likely to move from being a set of learning materials made up of lecture notes, to a set of learning materials made up of print, cassettes, disks and computer programs. Class contact hours will cease to be the major determinant of an academic workload. The teacher will then be released from being the sole source of information transmission and will become instead more a learning manager, able to pay attention to the development and delivery of education rather than to content.

Student-centred learning activities will also require innovative assessment strategies. Traditional assessment and reporting has aimed to produce a single mark or grade for each student. The mark is intended to indicate three things: the extent to which the learned material was mastered or understood; the level at which certain skills were performed, and the degree to which certain attitudes were displayed.

A deep learning approach would test a student's ability to identify and tackle new and unfamiliar 'real world' problems. A major assessment goal will be to increase the size and complexity of assignments and minimise what can be achieved by memorising or reproducing content. Wherever possible, students will be involved in the assessment process to assist them to learn how to make judgements about themselves and their work.

Questions 15 – 18

Do the following statements agree with the information given in Reading Passage 2?

In boxes 15-18 on your answer sheet, write

TRUE	*if the statement agrees with the information*
FALSE	*if the statement contradicts the information*
NOT GIVEN	*if there is no information on this*

15 Newman believed that the primary focus of universities was teaching.

16 Job promotion is already used to reward outstanding teaching.

17 Traditional approaches to assessment at degree level are having a negative effect on the learning process.

18 University students have complained about bad teaching and poor results.

Questions 19 – 23

*Look at the following statements (Questions 19-23) and the eight qualities of 'good teachers', **A-H**, in Reading Passage 2.*

*Match each statement with the correct quality, **A-H**.*

*Write the correct letter, **A-H**, in boxes 19-23 on your answer sheet.*

19 Good teachers can adapt their materials to different learning situations.

20 Good teachers assist students to understand the aims of the course.

21 Good teachers are interested in developing the students as learners.

22 Good teachers treat their students with dignity and concern.

23 Good teachers continually improve their teaching by monitoring their skills.

Questions 24 – 27

Choose the correct letter, **A**, **B**, **C** or **D**.

Write the correct letter in boxes 24-27 on your answer sheet.

24   In the future, university courses will focus more on

      A   developing students' skills and concepts.
      B   expanding students' knowledge.
      C   providing work experience for students.
      D   graduating larger numbers of students.

25   According to the author, university courses should prepare students to

      A   do a specific job well.
      B   enter traditional professions.
      C   change jobs easily.
      D   create their own jobs.

26   The author believes that new learning materials in universities will result in

      A   more work for teachers.
      B   a new role for teachers.
      C   more expensive courses.
      D   more choices for students.

27   The author predicts that university assessment techniques will include more

      A   in-class group assignments.
      B   theoretical exams.
      C   problem-solving activities.
      D   student seminar presentations.

READING PASSAGE 3

*You should spend about 20 minutes on **Questions 28-40**, which are based on Reading Passage 3.*

Questions 28 – 32

Reading Passage 3 has six sections, **A-F**.

*Choose the correct heading for sections **A-E** from the list of headings below.*

*Write the correct number, **i-x**, in boxes 28-32 on your answer sheet.*

List of Headings	
i	Contrary indications
ii	Europe's Alpine glaciers
iii	Growing consensus on sea level
iv	Ice cap observation
v	Causes of rising sea levels
vi	Panel on Climate Change
vii	Sea level monitoring difficulties
viii	Group response to alarming predictions
ix	Stockholm and Scandinavia
x	The world 130,000 years ago

28   Section **A**

29   Section **B**

30   Section **C**

31   Section **D**

32   Section **E**

Rising Sea Levels

A   During the night of 1st February 1953, a deadly combination of winds and tide raised the level of the North Sea, broke through the dykes which protected the Netherlands and inundated farmland and villages as far as 64 km from the coast, killing thousands. For people around the world who inhabit low-lying areas, variations in sea levels are of crucial importance and the scientific study of oceans has attracted increasing attention. Towards the end of the 1970s, some scientists began suggesting that global warming could cause the world's oceans to rise by several metres. The warming, they claimed, was an inevitable consequence of increasing carbon dioxide in the atmosphere, which acted like a greenhouse to trap heat in the air. The greenhouse warming was predicted to lead to rises in sea levels in a variety of ways. Firstly, heating the ocean water would cause it to expand. Such expansion might be sufficient to raise the sea level by 300mm in the next 100 years. Then there was the observation that in Europe's Alpine valleys glaciers had been shrinking for the past century. Meltwater from the mountain glaciers might have raised the oceans 50mm over the last 100 years and the rate is likely to increase in future. A third threat is that global warming might cause a store of frozen water in Antarctica to melt, which would lead to a calamitous rise in sea level of up to five metres.

B   The challenge of predicting how global warming will change sea levels led scientists of several disciplines to adopt a variety of approaches. In 1978 J H Mercer published a largely theoretical statement that a thick slab of ice covering much of West Antarctica is inherently unstable. He suggested that this instability meant that, given just 5 degrees Celsius of greenhouse warming in the south polar region, the floating ice shelves surrounding the West Antarctic ice sheet would begin to disappear. Without these buttresses, the grounded ice sheet would quickly disintegrate and coastlines around the world would be disastrously flooded. In evidence Mercer pointed out that between 130,000 and 110,000 years ago there had been just such a global warming as we have had in the past 20,000 years since the last ice age. In the geological remains of that earlier period there are indications that the sea level was five metres above the current sea level – just the level that would be reached if the West Antarctic ice sheet melted. The possibility of such a disastrous rise led a group of American investigators to form SeaRISE (Sea-level Response to Ice Sheet Evolution) in 1990. SeaRISE reported the presence of five active 'ice streams' drawing ice from the interior of West Antarctica into the Ross Sea. They stated that these channels in the West Antarctic ice sheet 'may be manifestations of collapse already under way'.

C   But doubt was cast on those dire warnings by the use of complex computer models of climate. Models of atmospheric and ocean behaviour predicted that greenhouse heating would cause warmer, wetter air to reach Antarctica, where it would deposit its moisture as snow. Thus, the sea ice surrounding the continent might even expand, causing sea levels to drop. Other observations have caused scientists working on Antarctica to doubt that sea levels will be pushed upward several metres by sudden melting. For example, glaciologists have discovered that one of the largest ice streams stopped moving about 130 years ago. Ellen Mosley-Thompson, questioning the SeaRISE theory, notes that ice streams 'seem to start and stop, and nobody really knows why'. Her own measurements of the rate of snow accumulation near the South Pole show that snowfalls have increased substantially in recent decades as global temperature has increased.

D   Most researchers are now willing to accept that human activities have contributed to global warming, but no one can say with any assurance whether the Antarctic ice cap is growing or shrinking in response. A satellite being planned by the National Aeronautics and Space Administration will use laser range finders to map changes in the elevation of the polar ice caps, perhaps to within 10 millimetres, and should end the speculation.

E   Whatever the fate of the polar ice caps may be, most researchers agree that the sea level is currently rising. That, however, is difficult to prove. Tide gauges in ports around the world have been measuring sea levels for decades, but the data are flawed because the land to which the gauges are attached can itself be moving up and down. In Stockholm the data from the sea level gauge show the sea level to be falling at four millimetres a year, but that is because all Scandinavia is still rebounding after being crushed by massive glaciers during the last ice age. By contrast, the gauge at Honolulu, which is more stable, shows the sea level to be rising at a rate of one and a half millimetres a year. Unstable regions cannot be omitted from the data because that would eliminate large areas of the world. Most of the eastern seaboard of North America is still settling after a great ice sheet which covered Eastern Canada 20,000 years ago tilted it up. And then there is buckling occurring at the edges of the great tectonic plates as they are pressed against each other. There is also land subsidence as oil and underground water is tapped. In Bangkok, for example, where the residents have been using groundwater, land subsidence makes it appear as if the sea has risen by almost a metre in the past 30 years.

F   Using complex calculations on the sea level gauge data, Peltier and Tushingham found that the global sea level has been rising at a rate of 2mm a year over the past few decades. Confirmation came from the TOPEX satellite, which used radar altimeters to calculate changes in ocean levels. Steven Nerem, working on the TOPEX data, found an average annual sea level rise of 2mm which is completely compatible with the estimates that have come from 50 years of tide gauge records. The key question still facing researchers is whether this trend will hold steady or begin to accelerate in response to a warming climate. The Intergovernmental Panel on Climate Change gives the broad prediction for the next century of a rise of between 200mm and 1 metre.

Questions 33 – 40

Complete each sentence with the correct ending, **A-L**, from the box below.

Write the correct letter, **A-L**, in boxes 33-40 on your answer sheet.

33   The Dutch dykes were broken

34   Without ice shelves, West Antarctic ice covers would contract

35   Mercer predicted a 5-metre sea-level rise

36   SeaRISE believed the collapse of Antarctic ice had begun

37   Mosley-Thompson doubted the SeaRISE theory

38   Doubts over Antarctica's trends will soon be settled

39   Stockholm's tide gauge shows a fall in sea level

40   At Bangkok the sea appears to have risen one metre in 30 years

A	because the land mass is rising.
B	because ice stream flows are variable and unpredictable.
C	because Europe's alpine valley glaciers were shrinking.
D	because of a combination of wind and high tide.
E	because of geological evidence of an earlier rise.
F	because satellites will take laser measurements.
G	because the temperature had risen five degrees in 1978.
H	because there were five active streams of ice.
I	because they are inherently unstable.
J	because use of groundwater has caused the land to sink.
K	because warmer, wetter air would increase snowfall.
L	because we cannot predict the rate of change.

Candidate Name _____

Candidate Number

[_____]

INTERNATIONAL ENGLISH LANGUAGE TESTING SYSTEM

ACADEMIC WRITING

PRACTICE MATERIALS   1 hour

Example 1

TIME   1 hour

INSTRUCTIONS TO CANDIDATES

Do not open this booklet until you are told to do so.

Write your name and candidate number in the spaces at the top of this page.

All answers must be written on the separate answer booklet provided.

Do not remove this booklet from the examination room.

INFORMATION FOR CANDIDATES

There are **2** tasks on this question paper.

You must do **both** tasks.

Underlength answers will be penalised.

WRITING TASK 1

You should spend about 20 minutes on this task.

The charts below show the number of Japanese tourists travelling abroad between 1985 and 1995 and Australia's share of the Japanese tourist market.

Summarise the information by selecting and reporting the main features, and make comparisons where relevant.

Write at least 150 words.

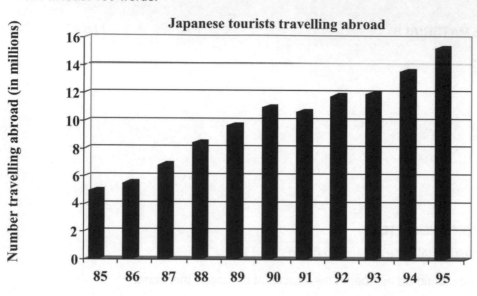

Japanese tourists travelling abroad

Australia's share of Japan's tourist market

WRITING TASK 2

You should spend about 40 minutes on this task.

Write about the following topic:

> *In many countries children are engaged in some kind of paid work.*
> *Some people regard this as completely wrong, while others consider it*
> *as valuable work experience, important for learning and taking*
> *responsibility.*
>
> **What are your opinions on this?**

Give reasons for your answer and include any relevant examples from your own knowledge
or experience.

Write at least 250 words.

Candidate Name _____

Candidate Number

INTERNATIONAL ENGLISH LANGUAGE TESTING SYSTEM

ACADEMIC WRITING

PRACTICE MATERIALS   1 hour

Example 2

TIME   1 hour

INSTRUCTIONS TO CANDIDATES

Do not open this booklet until you are told to do so.

Write your name and candidate number in the spaces at the top of this page.

All answers must be written on the separate answer booklet provided.

Do not remove this booklet from the examination room.

INFORMATION FOR CANDIDATES

There are **2** tasks on this question paper.

You must do **both** tasks.

Underlength answers will be penalised.

WRITING TASK 1

You should spend about 20 minutes on this task.

> *The diagrams below show some principles of house design for cool and for warm climates.*
>
> *Summarise the information by selecting and reporting the main features, and make comparisons where relevant.*

Write at least 150 words.

Cool Climate

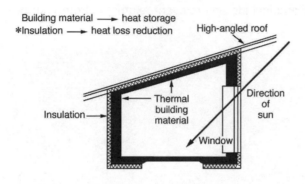

Warm Climate

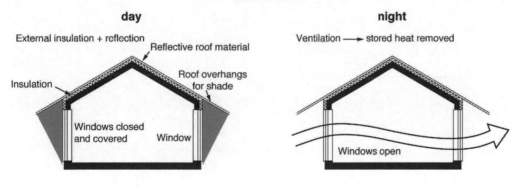

* Insulation – material used for building which prevents heat passing through it

WRITING TASK 2

You should spend about 40 minutes on this task.

Write about the following topic:

> *Many old buildings are protected by law because they are part of a nation's history. However, some people think old buildings should be knocked down to make way for new ones because people need houses and offices.*
>
> *How important is it to maintain old buildings?*
>
> *Should history stand in the way of progress?*

Give reasons for your answer and include any relevant examples from your own knowledge or experience.

Write at least 250 words.

Candidate Name _____

Candidate Number

INTERNATIONAL ENGLISH LANGUAGE TESTING SYSTEM

ACADEMIC WRITING

PRACTICE MATERIALS   1 hour

Example 3

TIME   1 hour

INSTRUCTIONS TO CANDIDATES

Do not open this booklet until you are told to do so.

Write your name and candidate number in the spaces at the top of this page.

All answers must be written on the separate answer booklet provided.

Do not remove this booklet from the examination room.

INFORMATION FOR CANDIDATES

There are **2** tasks on this question paper.

You must do **both** tasks.

Underlength answers will be penalised.

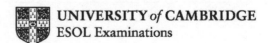

WRITING TASK 1

You should spend about 20 minutes on this task.

The graph below shows the number of complaints made about noise to Environmental Health authorities in the city of Newtown between 1980 and 1996.

Summarise the information by selecting and reporting the main features, and make comparisons where relevant.

Write at least 150 words.

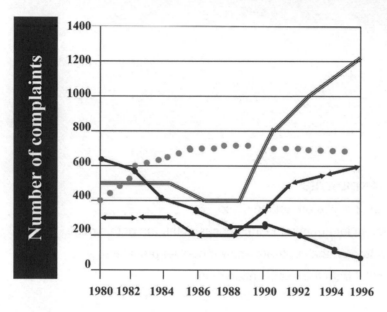

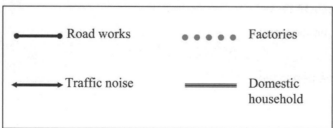

WRITING TASK 2

You should spend about 40 minutes on this task.

Write about the following topic:

> *Television is dangerous because it destroys family life and any sense of community; instead of visiting people or talking with our family we just watch television.*
>
> *To what extent do you agree or disagree with this opinion?*

Give reasons for your answer and include any relevant examples from your own knowledge or experience.

Write at least 250 words.

Candidate Name _____

Candidate Number

INTERNATIONAL ENGLISH LANGUAGE TESTING SYSTEM

GENERAL TRAINING READING

PRACTICE MATERIALS   1 hour

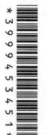

TIME   1 hour

INSTRUCTIONS TO CANDIDATES

Do not open this question booklet until you are told to do so.

Write your name and candidate number in the spaces at the top of this page.

Answer **all** questions.

Write your answers on the **separate answer sheet**. If you write your answers in the question booklet, you must copy them onto the separate answer sheet **within the time limit**.

Do not remove this booklet from the examination room.

INFORMATION FOR CANDIDATES

There are **40** questions in this question booklet. All questions carry one mark.

The test is divided into three sections.

  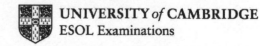

SECTION 1

Questions 1 – 14

Read the advertisements below and answer Questions 1-4.

A

Restaurant Supervisor

Waiting Staff

Telephonist

---

*The ideal candidates
must have relevant experience gained in
a high quality hotel. Please call Personnel on
020-7723-7723, or send your CV to: The
Aylesbury, Hodge Road, London SE1 8RS*

The Aylesbury
LONDON

B

USE YOUR
LANGUAGES AND EARN
£450-£1200 P.W.

We are one of the largest
business publishers in Europe
and have limited vacancies for
intelligent young people in our
London advertisement sales
office. Enquiries from German,
Spanish and Eastern European
speakers especially welcome.
Phone Steve Warburton on
020 7114 9610

C

SECRETARY

Busy Chartered Accountants require
experienced/efficient secretary. Accounts, typing
experience, and an excellent telephone manner
essential, shorthand useful.

**Please send CV to:
Box No. 9246
c/o Weekly Standard
Classified,
9 Berry Street,
Kensington W8 9LP**

D

TRAVEL
COMPANY
**Vacancy for self-confident person to look after
bookings for our Caribbean Hotels. Salary
based on applicant's experience & suitability.
Please send CV to
Greg Taplin, KRI Ltd,
12 Galena Road, London,
W6 3XZ**

E

NANNY WANTED
for 9 month old handful.
Artistic/Prof household
Notting Hill, 3 days per
week. Some hours
flexibility req'd.
Knowledge
German/Hungarian
advantage, not essential
020 7221 6119

F

Hollywood World
LONDON
Join the Stars!

Food Servers

The biggest and busiest restaurant in London is
seeking additional stars for its team of dedicated
professionals. If you have experience in high
volume restaurants and are looking for a challenge,
then come on down for an audition.
**Interview day is on Friday 6th May from
12 noon to 7pm.**

**Hollywood World is located at 29 Foster Street,
London W1 6JZ**

Questions 1 – 4

*Look at the six job advertisements, **A-F**.*

For which advertisement are the following statements true?

*Write the correct letter, **A-F**, in boxes 1-4 on your answer sheet.*

NB   *You may use any letter more than once.*

1   Which job is in a hotel?

2   Which job is for someone to look after a child?

3   Which **TWO** advertisements are for waiters?

4   Which **TWO** jobs would be particularly suitable for people who speak a language other than English?

Read the text below and answer Questions 5-10.

LIST OF TELEPHONE SERVICES

SERVICE	NUMBER TO DIAL
Operator Services	101

The operator is there to help you if you have difficulty making a call or if you want to use any of our special call services. These include: ALARM CALLS * ADVICE OF DURATION CHARGE * CREDIT CARD CALLS * FIXED TIME CALLS * FREEFONE CALLS * PERSONAL CALLS * TRANSFERRED CHARGE CALLS * SUBSCRIBER CONTROLLED TRANSFER. For details of charges see our free leaflet. Dial 101 and ask for financial services.

International Operator	123

See Section 3 (international) for details.

Directory Enquiries	142

Tell the operator the town you require. Have paper and pencil ready.

International Directory Enquiries	130

Emergency	010

Tell the operator what service you want.

Faults	166

Any fault should be reported to the local fault repair service.

Sales	170

For enquiries regarding other purchases.

Telemessage	190

If you have something special to say and prefer to say it in writing.

International Telemessage	191

International Telegrams	192

You can send a telegram to most other countries.

Maritime Services	200

SHIP'S TELEGRAM SERVICE * SHIP'S TELEPHONE SERVICE * INMARSAT SATELLITE SERVICE. You can call or send a message to someone aboard ship by using our Maritime Services. For telephone calls to ships quote the name of the Coast Radio Station if known. For INMARSAT (Maritime Satellite) service dial 178. Give the ship's name, its identification number and ocean region, if known. International Directory Enquiries, code 130, can say if a ship is equipped for satellite service and provide the number.

Any Other Call Enquiries	111

Questions 5 – 10

Answer the questions below.

Write the correct telephone numbers in boxes 5-10 on your answer sheet.

NB   *You may use any number more than once.*

What number should you dial if

5   there is something wrong with your telephone?

6   there has been an accident and you want to call an ambulance?

7   you want to find out a number in a foreign country?

8   you want to know how much telephone calls cost?

9   you want to buy an answer-phone machine?

10   you want to use a credit card to pay for a telephone call?

Read the text below and answer Questions 11-14.

FIRE NOTICE

In the event of fire, the ALARM will ring. On hearing the fire alarm, all those in the West Wing should evacuate the building by staircase J. Rooms 1 to 199 are in the West Wing. All others should use staircase A. The assembly area for occupants of the West Wing is the staff car park at the rear of the building. All others assemble in the courtyard.

Evacuate the building even if the alarm stops.

If you discover a fire, shout "FIRE" and operate the nearest fire alarm. Attack the fire with an extinguisher but do not take any risks. Inform reception by dialling 3333.

Questions 11– 14

Answer the questions below.

*Choose **NO MORE THAN THREE WORDS** from the text for each answer.*

Write your answers in boxes 11-14 on your answer sheet.

11   You are in room 101. Which staircase should you use to evacuate the building?

12   You are in room 201. Where should you wait outside after evacuating the building?

13   What should you do if the alarm stops?

14   Who should you contact if you discover a fire?

SECTION 2   Questions 15 – 27

Read the text below and answer Questions 15-20.

✍📖 *HILTON ENGLISH LANGUAGE CENTRE* 📖✍
INFORMATION FOR NEW STUDENTS

CLASS TIMES

9.00am – 10.30am   11.00am – 12.30pm   1.30pm – 3.00pm

The Language Centre is open Monday to Friday. Each class has one afternoon
free per week, but lessons on the other four. On the first day go to the
lecture hall to check your timetable.

SELF-ACCESS

The language laboratory (Room 1110) is open Monday to Friday from 3.15pm to
5.00pm for all full-time students. You can learn how to use the computers for
language games or word-processing.

There are cassettes for students to borrow to practise their English. Go in
and ask the assistant to show you.

If you plan to take public examinations, there are dictation and listening
comprehension cassettes for you to practise with. There are cloze exercises
on the computers. Ask your class teacher for a list of past exam essays.
Students can borrow cassettes to take home but they must be returned after two
days.

ATTENDANCE

All students on student visas are expected to attend classes regularly.
Students who do not attend classes will be reported to OSS. Eighty per cent
attendance is required for students to receive their certificate on completion
of their course. It is also required by OSS for an extension to your visa.

BOOKS

If students are given course books, the books are their responsibility. If a
book is lost, the student will be expected to pay for it. If students wish to
buy books, there is a bookshop in the college specialising in English books
(Room 3520).

Questions 15 – 20

Answer the questions below.

Choose **NO MORE THAN THREE WORDS AND/OR NUMBERS** *from the text for each answer.*

Write your answers in boxes 15-20 on your answer sheet.

15 When do classes begin and end on a full day?

16 How many afternoons does a class meet each week?

17 Where are the timetables displayed?

18 Who can use the language laboratory after classes?

19 Who is available in the self-access centre to help the students?

20 How much of a course must you attend according to visa restrictions?

Read the text below and answer Questions 21-27.

The College

The college has the advantage of location in one of the most attractive cities in the country. Within the city of Bath it occupies modern buildings in a landscaped garden on Sion Hill, Lansdown and an adjacent Georgian crescent, Somerset Crescent, which includes teaching and residential accommodation for post-graduate studies. It also occupies three houses in Sydney Place, which are used for studio and workshop accommodation for part-time courses in the Visual Arts and for the Foundation Course in Art and Design.

The Newton Park site is situated four miles west of Bath between the villages of Newton St Loe and Corston. Within the grounds are a Georgian mansion, where the college's Central Administration is located, an Elizabethan dairy, stables and the tower of a medieval manor house; all these older buildings have been adapted to present-day use. A new purpose-built Home Economics Block was opened in January 2007. During 2008 a new Sports Hall will be completed and new residential blocks are under construction to be completed ready for the start of the academic year in September 2008; a new Music Block will be completed in 2009.

The Art and Design degree courses which are currently accommodated at Corsham, about nine miles east of Bath, will be moved to the Sion Hill site in Bath by September 2008 thus reinforcing faculty and course links.

The college courses are designed to take advantage of the special opportunities and circumstances provided by its environment. Students have available such resources as the Costume and Fashion Research Centre, the Royal Photographic Centre and the Museum of American Domestic Life at Claverton. Concerts and recitals, including some given by staff and students, take place throughout the year in the Assembly Rooms.

Questions 21 – 27

The college uses five different locations.

Classify the following buildings and courses as being located in

        A   *Newton Park*
        B   *Corsham*
        C   *Sion Hill*
        D   *Somerset Crescent*
        E   *Sydney Place*

*Write the correct letter, **A-E**, in boxes 21-27 on your answer sheet.*

NB   *You may use any letter more than once.*

21   Central Administration

22   Home Economics Block

23   Art and Design Foundation Course

24   Art and Design degree courses after 2008

25   Post-graduate residences

26   Sports Hall

27   Music Block

WINTER
SPORTS

Ice,

danger

and

exhilaration

The 17th Winter Games, held in Norway in 1994, were part of an Olympic tradition which goes back almost 3,000 years. For more than 1,000 years the ancient Games were held, every four years, on hallowed ground near Mount Olympus, where the Greek gods were said to live.

The 'Olympics' brought together men from war-torn tribes and states in Greece and its colonies. A sacred truce was declared to allow men to travel to the games in safety. Women could not take part and were forbidden, on pain of death, even to attend the Games.

The ancient Olympics were abolished by the Roman Emperor Theodosius in 393 AD, after Greece had lost its independence. But the idea never died and the Frenchman Baron Pierre de Coubertin, an educator and scholar, founded the modern Olympics. His aim was to bring together, once every four years, athletes from all countries on the friendly fields of amateur sport. No account was to be taken of national rivalries, nor politics, race, religion, wealth or social status.

The first modern Games were held in Athens in 1896, and four years later, in Paris, women began to take part. Although the Winter Olympics did not begin until 1924, individual figure skating was part of the 1908 London Summer Olympics; both skating and ice hockey were successfully included in the Antwerp Games in 1920. But generally winter sports were felt to be too specialised. Only cold-weather countries had much experience of activities such as skiing – a means of transport overland across ice and snow during long winters.

The Scandinavians, for whom skiing is a part of everyday life, had objected to a Winter Games. They feared it would threaten their own Nordic Games, which had been held every four years since 1901. But the International Olympic Committee (IOC) agreed to stage an International Sports Week in Chamonix, France, in 1924. It was a success and the Scandinavians won 28 of the 43 medals, including nine golds. They dropped their objections and the event was retrospectively named the First Olympic Winter Games.

Apart from the Second World War period the Winter Olympics were held every four years, a few months before the Summer Olympics. But in 1986 the IOC changed the schedule so that the Summer and Winter Games would be held in different years. Thus, for the only time in history, the Lillehammer (Norway) Games took place just two years after the previous Winter Olympics, which were held in Albertville, France.

Since the Winter Games began, 55 out of 56 gold medals in the men's nordic skiing events have been won by competitors from Scandinavia or the former Soviet Union. For teams from warm weather countries, cross-country skiing can pose problems. At the Calgary Games in 1988, one competitor in the 50-kilometre event was so slow that race officials feared he was lost and sent out a search party. Roberto Alvarez of Mexico had never skied more than 20 kilometres before and finished 61st and last – 52 minutes behind the 60th place.

Questions 28 – 32

Complete the table below.

Choose **NO MORE THAN ONE NUMBER** from the text for each answer.

Write your answers in boxes 28-32 on your answer sheet.

YEAR	EVENT
28	Ancient Olympics came to an end
29	First women's events
30	First Nordic Games
31	First winter team game included in Olympics
32	First Winter Olympic Games

Questions 33 – 40

Do the following statements agree with the information given in the text?

In boxes 33-40 on your answer sheet, write

    TRUE   if the statement agrees with the information
    FALSE   if the statement contradicts the information
    NOT GIVEN if there is no information on this

33   The spectators of the ancient Olympics, as well as the participants, were all male.

34   Only amateur athletes are allowed to compete in the modern Olympics.

35   The modern Olympics have always demonstrated the political neutrality intended by their founder.

36   The Antwerp Games proved that winter sports were too specialised.

37   One Winter Olympics has succeeded another every four years since 1924 with a break only for the Second World War.

38   The French Winter Olympics took place in 1992.

39   Only Scandinavians have won gold medals in men's Winter Olympics Nordic skiing events.

40   Cross-country skiing events are a speciality of cold-weather countries.

INTERNATIONAL ENGLISH LANGUAGE TESTING SYSTEM

GENERAL TRAINING WRITING

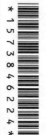

PRACTICE MATERIALS   1 hour

Example 1

TIME   1 hour

INSTRUCTIONS TO CANDIDATES

Do not open this booklet until you are told to do so.

Write your name and candidate number in the spaces at the top of this page.

All answers must be written on the separate answer booklet provided.

Do not remove this booklet from the examination room.

INFORMATION FOR CANDIDATES

There are **2** tasks on this question paper.

You must do **both** tasks.

Underlength answers will be penalised.

© UCLES 2007

WRITING TASK 1

You should spend about 20 minutes on this task.

> *You have just started a course in a college which has no sports facilities of its own.*
>
> *Write a letter to the manager of the nearest private sports club. In your letter*
>
> - *introduce yourself*
> - *say why you are interested in this sports club*
> - *ask some questions about the club (e.g. facilities, members, costs)*

Write at least 150 words.

You do **NOT** need to write any addresses.

Begin your letter as follows:

Dear Sir or Madam,

WRITING TASK 2

You should spend about 40 minutes on this task.

Write about the following topic:

> *In many countries people no longer wear their national costumes. They
> are forgetting their history and traditions. More people should be
> encouraged to wear their national costumes every day.*
>
> *Do you agree or disagree?*

Give reasons for your answer and include any relevant examples from your own knowledge
or experience.

Write at least 250 words.

Candidate Name _____

Candidate Number

INTERNATIONAL ENGLISH LANGUAGE TESTING SYSTEM

GENERAL TRAINING WRITING

PRACTICE MATERIALS   1 hour

Example 2

TIME   1 hour

INSTRUCTIONS TO CANDIDATES

Do not open this booklet until you are told to do so.

Write your name and candidate number in the spaces at the top of this page.

All answers must be written on the separate answer booklet provided.

Do not remove this booklet from the examination room.

INFORMATION FOR CANDIDATES

There are **2** tasks on this question paper.

You must do **both** tasks.

Underlength answers will be penalised.

WRITING TASK 1

You should spend about 20 minutes on this task.

> *You recently bought a large expensive item but when it was delivered to your home you found some problems with it.*
>
> *Write a letter to the manager of the shop. In your letter*
>
> - *give details of what you bought*
> - *describe the problems with your item*
> - *say what you want the shop to do*

Write at least 150 words.

You do **NOT** need to write your any addresses.

Begin your letter as follows:

Dear Sir or Madam,

WRITING TASK 2

You should spend about 40 minutes on this task.

Write about the following topic:

> *People should be allowed to continue to work for as long as they want to, and not be forced to retire at a particular age such as 60 or 65.*
>
> *Do you agree or disagree?*

Give reasons for your answer and include any relevant examples from your own knowledge or experience.

Write at least 250 words.

SPEAKING

The Speaking test takes between 11 and 14 minutes. It consists of an oral interview between one candidate and an examiner.

There are three parts. Each part is different in terms of the type of interaction, the task input and the type of response.

In **Part 1** candidates answer general questions about themselves, their homes/families, their jobs/studies, their interests, and a range of similar familiar topic areas. This part lasts between four and five minutes.

In **Part 2** the candidate is given a task card and is asked to talk on a particular topic. The candidate has one minute to prepare before speaking for up to two minutes. The examiner then asks one or two rounding-off questions.

In **Part 3** the examiner and candidate engage in a discussion of more abstract issues and ideas which are related to the topic prompt in Part 2. The discussion lasts between four and five minutes.

All interviews are recorded.

Structure of the Speaking test

Part	Nature of interaction	Timing
Part 1 Introduction and interview	Examiner introduces him/herself and confirms candidate's identity. Examiner interviews candidate using verbal questions selected from familiar topic frames.	4-5 minutes
Part 2 Individual long turn	Examiner asks candidate to speak for 1-2 minutes on a particular topic based on written input in the form of a candidate task card with content-focused prompts. Examiner asks one or two questions to round off the long turn.	3-4 minutes (including 1 minute preparation time)
Part 3 Two-way discussion	Examiner invites candidate to participate in discussion of a more abstract nature, based on questions thematically linked to Part 2 topic.	4-5 minutes

Speaking Test Practice Materials

Part One

Let's talk about where you grew up.

- Describe the town or city where you grew up.
- Do you still live there now?
- Does your family still live there?
- Do you think the place has changed much since you were young? [How?]

Part Two
Candidate task card:

Describe a sports event you enjoyed watching.

    You should say:

        what event you watched
        where you were
        who you watched it with

and explain why you enjoyed watching it.

You will have to talk about the topic for 1 to 2 minutes.

You have one minute to think about what you're going to say.

You can make some notes to help you if you wish.

Rounding-off questions:

- Who won this event?
- Do you play this sport yourself?

Part Three

Let's consider first of all watching sport …

- How expensive is it to go to sports events in your country?
- Do you think it's different watching a sports event on TV and going to watch it in person? In what ways?
- Do you think there's too much sport on TV? Why?

Finally, let's talk about famous sports people …

- Why do you think sports people often become media stars today?

How to mark the Listening and Reading Practice Tests

General points

Put a tick (✔) next to each correct answer and a cross (✗) next to each wrong one. Each tick will equal one mark.

Single letter/number answers

1. For questions where the answer is a single letter or number, you should have written only one answer. If you have written more than one, the answer must be marked wrong.

2. Candidates may use upper or lower case in writing their answers, but they should take care to write the letters clearly, as any unclear letters are marked as wrong.

Longer answers

1. Sometimes part of the correct answer is given in brackets. Words in brackets are optional – they are correct, but not necessary. If you have written any other extra words that are not on the key, your answer must be marked as wrong.

2. Sometimes there are alternative correct answers to a question. In these cases the possible answers are separated by a slash (/), e.g. questions 34, 35, etc. in the Listening test. If you have written any one of these possible answers, your answer is correct.

3. You will find additional notes about individual questions in the answer keys themselves.

4. Answers may be written in upper or lower case.

Spelling

1. Candidates should take care when writing their answers on the Answer Sheets as incorrect spelling and grammar are penalised.

2. All answers including words in brackets require correct spelling. If a word is spelt differently from the answer key, it should be marked wrong.

3. Both UK and US varieties of spelling are accepted and are included in the answer keys.

Interpreting your Scores

In interpreting your scores, there are a number of points you should bear in mind.

1. Your performance in the real IELTS test will be reported in two ways: there will be a Band Score from 1 to 9 for each of the skills; and an Overall Band Score from 1 to 9, which is the average of your scores in the four skills. For example, if you score Band 6 for Listening, Band 6 for Reading, Band 5 for Writing and Band 7 for Speaking, your Overall Band Score will be:

$$\frac{6+6+5+7}{4} = \frac{24}{4} = 6$$

You will see from this example that a lower score in one test can be compensated for by good scores in the others.

2. Institutions or bodies considering your application are advised to look at both the Overall Band and the Bands for each skill. They do this in order to see if you have the language skills needed for a particular purpose. For example, if your course has a lot of reading and writing, but no lectures, listening comprehension might not be very important and a score of, say, 5 in Listening might be acceptable if the Overall Band Score was 7. However, for a course where there are lots of lectures and spoken instructions, a score of 5 in Listening might be unacceptable even though the Overall Band Score was 7.

3. Once you have marked your papers you should have some idea of whether your Listening and Reading skills are good enough for you to try the real IELTS test. If you did well enough in one test but not in the others, you will have to decide for yourself whether you are ready to take the real test yet.

4. This Practice Test has been checked so that it is about the same level of difficulty as the real IELTS test. However, we cannot guarantee that your score in the Practice Test will be reflected in the real IELTS test. The Practice Test can only give you an idea of your possible future performance and it is ultimately up to you to make decisions based on your practice score.

5. Different institutions or bodies accept different IELTS scores for different types of courses. We have based our recommendations on the average scores which the majority of institutions accept. The institution to which you are applying may, of course, require a higher or lower score than most other institutions. Please check score requirements for individual institutes on the IELTS website **www.ielts.org**

Listening Answer Key

Your score in Listening

Scores 25 and above

If you have strictly followed the guidelines on page iii you are likely to get an acceptable score on the IELTS Listening test under examination conditions, but remember that different institutions will find different scores acceptable (see point 5 on page 52).

Scores 16–24

You may not get an acceptable score on the IELTS Listening test under examination conditions and we recommend that you think about having more lessons or practice before you take IELTS.

Scores 0–15

You are highly unlikely to get an acceptable score on the IELTS Listening test under examination conditions and we recommend that you spend a lot of time improving your English before you apply to take IELTS.

Listening Answer Key

Each question correctly answered scores 1 mark.

Section 1 **Questions 1–10**

1	G
2	C
3	C
4	B
5	A
6	A (and) E *(in either order; both required for 1 mark)*
7	slim
8	black
9	35
10	(small) scar

Section 2 **Questions 11–20**

11	C
12	B
13	C
14 & 15	A D *(in either order)*
16	75
17	evening(s)
18	(four-course) dinner
19	52
20	golf club

Section 3 **Questions 21–30**

21	A+/plus
22	lecture
23	B
24	pink slip
25	department(al)
26	Information Desk
27	25p/pence
28	summarise/summarize
29	essay plan(s)
30	(give) feedback

Section 4 **Questions 31–40**

31	Australia
32	(flight/flying) speed / speed of flight
33	looking/searching for food
34	start/begin to fly / start/begin flying
35	full/adult size / full adult size / full(y) grown
36	leave (the/their) nest(s)
37	die
38	attach (identification/ID/aluminium/aluminum) rings
39	note (the) sex
40	(general) health

Listening Tapescript

SECTION 1

You will hear a woman called Mrs Reynolds being interviewed by a police officer about an incident she saw the previous evening.

M: Well, if you can just tell me everything you remember. It doesn't matter how trivial it seems. What may seem unimportant to you may not be unimportant to us.

F: OK, I'll do what I can, officer. Well, as I said, I'd just come out of the cinema on the High Street, so it was about 8 o'clock. Just before eight in fact. I'd been to see a film with a friend and she'd just gone off home. So I was just standing there wondering what to do, whether to go and have a cup of coffee somewhere or not. I was just standing there minding my own business when I suddenly heard someone shouting directly opposite me outside the library. Not screaming, just shouting. It sounded like the voice of an elderly woman. "They've got my bag! They've got my bag!", she was shouting. Then these two men raced past me, going like the wind, straight down the street and round the corner into West Street. It all happened so quickly I think they must have had a car waiting for them there because I heard one drive off at top speed. Well, I didn't know what on earth to do; whether to try and chase them, whether to ring the police or whether to go and see if she was all right. Another woman was running up behind me so I shouted back at her to go and call the police. Anyway, when I got to the woman, she seemed to be all right, thank goodness. A bit shaken, but OK. I think I was much more upset than she was.

All in all, she was pretty calm. I don't think I would have been, but apparently it had happened to her once before so maybe that's why. You know, I've got a friend who refuses to go out alone anywhere after six o'clock now. What's this town coming to?

Well, anyway, she just kept saying, "I didn't see a thing, I didn't see a thing". One of them had just pushed her from behind and as she put out her hand to steady herself, the other one had just taken the bag from under her arm. And then he raced off across the road. I asked her what she'd had in it, and she said she'd had her purse with about £15 in it, but no cheque book or cards or things like that. And luckily she had her front door key in her pocket. Oh, and she'd had her bus pass taken too.

M: Let's get back to the two men, if we can. Just tell me everything you can remember about them.

F: Well, there was a younger one and an older one.

M: Well, let's start with the younger one, shall we?

F: Well, age first then. He only looked about 17 – not more. Something like that. Neither very tall nor small. Sort of slim build. Not anybody you'd notice. Nothing particularly special about him. An ordinary looking sort of bloke. He had curly black hair which was quite long. But apart from that, as I say, not someone you'd notice in a crowd. Nothing really distinct about him at all. But the other one, the older one, he was different.

M: Different?

F: Yes, different. I feel as if I'd know him anywhere again. I got more of a look at him because he ran across the road more slowly than the younger man. I remember being surprised because he was quite a bit older than the other one. I'd say about 35. Funny, because you don't think of people of that age snatching handbags in broad daylight like that, do you? He was quite a bit smaller than the other man. And medium build.

M: What did he look like? You didn't give the officer much information last night.

F: Well, I did get quite a good look at his face. No beard or moustache – clean shaven and quite smart-looking really. He had light brown hair cut very short. A sort of army haircut. And there was another thing. Thinking about it all last night over and over again, I'm almost sure he had a small scar on his chin. I didn't tell the other policeman that last night, but in my mind each time I see his face, I can see one.

M: A scar on his chin? That could be important. Thank you, Mrs Reynolds. You've been really helpful. If you really think you'd recognise him again, then what we'd like you to do later this morning, if you can, is to come down to the police station and look at a few photographs for us.

SECTION 2

You will hear a recorded message giving information about an English hotel.

Welcome to the Bridge Hotel Information Line. The Bridge Hotel is part of the Compact Group, which is a large association of family-owned hotels offering a warm friendly atmosphere and high quality service at competitive prices. All of them cater for a wide range of people – from business to leisure clients.

Set in a quiet residential area on the attractive outskirts of Belford, about three miles from the city centre, the Bridge Hotel is a popular choice for conferences. After recent refurbishment and expansion, it now has 25 double rooms and 20 singles. All 45 are en suite with TV and coffee- and tea-making facilities.

The Bridge Hotel is set in three and a half hectares of grounds with an open-air swimming pool and four tennis courts. There is also a newly opened gym with fitness suite, which is considered one of the best equipped in the area. Non-resident membership is available.

We have a fully licensed restaurant for residents and non-residents, which provides a wide range of dishes with a particular focus on dishes from around the world.

For the discerning business customer, we have designated business rooms with phone links allowing full internet access. Our conference facilities cater for up to 200 delegates and we are able to offer transport to guests to and from Birmingham Airport at a small extra cost.

There now follows information about short break packages.

Welcome to the Bridge Hotel Short Breaks Information Line. We offer three packages:

2-day, 3-day and 5-day.

The 2-day break costs £75 per person per night and includes full cooked breakfast and evening entertainment. Very popular for weekend getaways.

The 3-day break costs £60 per person per night and in addition to offers for the 2-day break, includes one four-course dinner. This allows guests to enjoy the full range of hotel facilities.

The 5-day break costs £52 per person per night and, in addition to offers from the 2- and 3-day breaks, includes free beauty therapy on two days and a full-day pass to a golf club. This package is particularly popular with couples who want a completely relaxing break.

If you would like more information about these special packages, call Extension 3469 to speak to our Customer Service Manager, John Martin.

Thank you for calling the Bridge Hotel Information Line.

SECTION 3

You will hear three students talking about their study programmes.

M: Hi, Elaine, I was hoping I'd see you here. How're things?

F1: All right. You?

M: Not bad, but I'm beginning to worry about that assignment.

F1: What, the one on Theory and Practice?

M: Yes.

F1: When's it got to be in by?

M: Next Thursday, and I just can't get to grips with it.

F1: Yes, it's a tricky one. I'm hoping to get down to it over the weekend. I tell you what, there's Dina. Let's see if she has any pearls of wisdom on the subject. She took the Theory and Practice option last year, didn't she? And got an A+ for it, I think.

M: How does she do it?

F1: Let's ask her. Hi, Dina. Hard at work?

F2: Not exactly. The lecture's just been cancelled, so I've suddenly got a free morning on my hands.

F1: That's lucky. You've met Neil, haven't you?

F2: Yes.

F1: We were just talking about the Theory and Practice assignment we've got to hand in next. Can we just pick your brains a moment?

F2: How far have you got with it?

F1: Well, still at the reading stage really.

F2: Are you? Well, one bit of advice I'd definitely give is not to spend hours wading through that massive volume by Jespersen; it really isn't very helpful – I think the only reason they keep it on the reading list is that the library has got so many copies of it. Personally, I found the essential source was Piresi; have you read her yet?

F1: Piresi? I don't think so.

F2: That's a great book, it must be on your reading list.

M: Right.

F2: Another one I found very useful was the article called something like 'Practical theories', by, was it Williams? Or Willard. Yes, Willard. Also, if you want to look at case studies, that small book of Ron Brown's has got some interesting stuff in - you know the one I mean?

M: Ron Brown, yes. I looked for it in the library but it was out on loan.

F2: Yes it's a very popular book. Did you try the recall system?

M: The what?

F2: Don't you use the recall system? You should, you know. You just have to take a pink slip from any of the librarians' desks, fill the details of the book in, put your departmental address on the back – your departmental address not your home address – and hand the slip in at the Information Desk. Then check the mail in your department twice a day, say at 10 in the morning and three in the afternoon, for a slip telling you the book is ready to collect. Last week I recalled a book at lunch-time and got the slip telling me it was ready just 4 hours later. That was exceptional: it usually takes about three days.

M: I didn't know you could do that. Is it expensive?

F2: No, there's a nominal charge – 25 pence a book, I think. It's well worth it if you're preparing for an assignment. Are you going to be working together on it?

M: Erm, I'm not sure.

F2: I would, if I were you. You get so much more out of the assignment that way.

M: But surely the tutors would notice that our essays were the same?

F2: No, no. I'm certainly not suggesting you should actually write the thing together. I'm talking about when you first start on a big assignment. I think it's a good idea to find two or three others on the course who live near you, and divide up the reading-load between you. Then you can meet up again a few days later and take it in turns to summarise your reading for each other. At the next stage we go round the group explaining our essay-plans, which makes it easier for individuals then to go off and write the first draft of their essay on their own. Later on we usually exchange drafts and give feedback in the group, before finally writing our essays individually.

M: Do you really do all that?

F2: Usually, yes. It makes the whole thing much easier and more enjoyable.

M: Right. Well, I think I need another coffee before getting started. Can I get you one?

F2: Yes, why not.

SECTION 4

You will hear a talk by a university lecturer in Australia on a type of bird called a peregrine falcon.

I'm Professor Sam Richards, and I've come as the third guest lecturer on this course in Australian birds of prey. My job is to keep a watchful scientific eye on the state of Tasmanian peregrines, so I'll start by giving you some background to these magnificent birds of prey before I speak briefly on my own project.

Peregrine falcons are found on all continents with the exception of Antarctica. So don't go looking for them at the South Pole. They are found almost everywhere in Australia and it's interesting to note that the name, peregrine, implies that they are wanderers – that they move from place to place following the seasons – and indeed, in most parts of the world they are migratory birds. But not in Australia, however, where they prefer to stay in one place.

They are known to be the world's fastest creature and they have been tracked by radar diving down towards the ground at 180 km an hour. However, a number of textbooks claim that their flight speed can go as high as 350 km an hour, so there is still some dispute about just how fast they can actually fly.

Female peregrine falcons, like all other Australian falcons, are larger than their male counterparts; in fact the female is almost a third larger than the male in the case of peregrines. While she stays close to the nest to protect the eggs and the young chicks, the male is mostly occupied looking for food.

Peregrines typically lay two or three eggs per nest and, after the eggs have hatched, when the chicks are about 20 days old, they start to fly. So they fly at a very young age. By the time they are just 28 days old, they have already reached full adult size; in other words, they are fully grown. Soon after this, at about two months after hatching from the egg, they leave the nest for good. From this point on they are on their own. Unlike their parents, which have learned how to hunt, the young falcons are not good at feeding themselves and so during the first year about 60% of them die. Once the birds have managed to live to breeding age, at two years old, they generally go on to live for another six or seven years.

When we come across nests with young chicks, the first thing we do is catch the chicks before they are able to fly. We have to catch them at an early age. We then attach identification rings to their legs. These rings are made of colour-coded aluminium and they allow us to identify the birds through binoculars later in their lives. Thirdly, because we need to know how many males and how many female chicks are being born, we note the sex of the chicks. Noting the sex of the birds is a vital part of our research, as I will discuss later. The next thing to do is to take a blood sample from the chicks. We take the blood sample so that we can check the level of pesticide in their bodies. Peregrine falcons can build dangerous quantities of pesticides in their blood stream by feeding on smaller mammals which in turn feed on crops, grown on farms where pesticides are used. Finally we check the birds thoroughly, really checking the birds for their general health. This whole process only takes a few minutes; in fact, most of our time in the field is actually spent trying to find the nests, not on the data collection itself.

Well, that's all I have for you today. If you'd like to do some further reading …

Academic Reading Answer Key

Your score in Academic Reading

Scores 26 and above
If you have strictly followed the guidelines on page iii you are likely to get an acceptable score on the IELTS Academic Reading test under examination conditions, but remember that different institutions will find different scores acceptable (see point 5 on page 52).

Scores 17–25
You may not get an acceptable score on the IELTS Academic Reading test under examination conditions and we recommend that you should think about having more lessons or practice before you take IELTS.

Scores 0–16
You are highly unlikely to get an acceptable score on the IELTS Academic Reading test under examination conditions and we recommend that you spend a lot of time improving your English before you apply to take IELTS.

Academic Reading Answer Key

Each question correctly answered scores 1 mark.

Section 1	Questions 1–14		Section 3	Questions 28–40
1	E		28	v
2	H		29	viii
3	I		30	i
4	D		31	iv
5	G		32	vii
6 & 7	yeast bacteria *(in either order)*		33	D
			34	I
8	protein		35	E
9	chemical solvents		36	H
10	(small) holes		37	B
11	(the/a) (solid) fibre/fiber		38	F
12	FALSE		39	A
13	TRUE		40	J
14	NOT GIVEN			

Section 2	Questions 15–27
15	TRUE
16	FALSE
17	TRUE
18	NOT GIVEN
19	C
20	G
21	D
22	H
23	A
24	A
25	C
26	B
27	C

General Training Reading Answer Key

Your score in General Training Reading

Scores 24 and above

If you have strictly followed the guidelines on page iii you are likely to get an acceptable score on the IELTS General Training Reading test under examination conditions, but remember that different institutions will find different scores acceptable (see point 5 on page 52).

Scores 16–23

You may not get an acceptable score on the IELTS General Training Reading test under examination conditions and we recommend that you should think about having more lessons or practice before you take IELTS.

Scores 0–15

You are highly unlikely to get an acceptable score on the IELTS General Training Reading test under examination conditions and we recommend that you spend a lot of time improving your English before you apply to take IELTS.

General Training Reading Answer Key

Each question correctly answered scores 1 mark.

Section 1	Questions 1–14		Section 3	Questions 28–40
1	A		28	393
2	E		29	1900
3	A (and) F *(in either order; both required for 1 mark)*		30	1901
			31	1920
4	B (and) E *(in either order; both required for 1 mark)*		32	1924
5	166		33	TRUE
6	010		34	NOT GIVEN
7	130		35	NOT GIVEN
8	101		36	FALSE
9	170		37	FALSE
10	101		38	TRUE
11	(staircase) J		39	FALSE
12	(in) (the) courtyard		40	TRUE
13	evacuate (the building)			
14	(the) reception			

Section 2   Questions 15–27

15	9.00/nine am (and) 3.00/three pm
16	4/four
17	(the) lecture hall/room
18	(all) full-time students
19	(an/the) assistant
20	eighty per cent/80%
21	A
22	A
23	E
24	C
25	D
26	A
27	A

How Writing is assessed: Sample Candidate Writing Scripts and Examiner Comment

Both the Academic and General Training Writing tests consist of two tasks, Task 1 and Task 2. Each task is assessed independently. The assessment of Task 2 carries more weight in marking than Task 1.

Detailed performance descriptors have been developed which describe written performance at the nine IELTS bands. These descriptors are confidential and apply to both the Academic and General Training tests.

Task 1 scripts are assessed on the following criteria:

- Task Achievement
- Coherence and Cohesion
- Lexical Resource
- Grammatical Range and Accuracy

Task 2 scripts are assessed on the following criteria:

- Task Response
- Coherence and Cohesion
- Lexical Resource
- Grammatical Range and Accuracy

Candidates should note that scripts will be penalised if they are a) under the minimum word length, b) partly or wholly plagiarised, c) not written as full, connected text (e.g. using bullet points in any part of the response, or note form, etc.).

Task 1

Task Achievement

This criterion assesses how appropriately, accurately and relevantly the response fulfils the requirements set out in the task, using the minimum of 150 words.

Academic Writing Task 1 is a writing task which has a defined input and a largely predictable output. It is basically an information-transfer task which relates narrowly to the factual content of an input diagram and not to speculated explanations that lie outside the given data.

General Training Writing Task 1 is also a writing task with a largely predictable output in that each task sets out the context and purpose of the letter and the functions the candidate should cover in order to achieve this purpose.

Coherence and Cohesion

This criterion is concerned with the overall clarity and fluency of the message: how the response organises and links information, ideas and language. Coherence refers to the linking of ideas through logical sequencing. Cohesion refers to the varied and appropriate use of cohesive devices (for example, logical connectors, pronouns and conjunctions) to assist in making the conceptual and referential relationships between and within sentences clear.

Lexical Resource

This criterion refers to the range of vocabulary the candidate has used and the accuracy and appropriacy of that use in terms of the specific task.

Grammatical Range and Accuracy

This criterion refers to the range and accurate use of the candidate's grammatical resource as manifested in the candidate's writing at sentence level.

Task 2

Task Response

In both Academic and General Training tests Task 2 requires the candidates to formulate and develop a position in relation to a given prompt in the form of a question or statement. Ideas should be supported by evidence, and examples may be drawn from the candidate's own experience. Responses must be at least 250 words in length.

The final Writing score is reported as a whole band or half band.

Writing scripts are assessed by certificated examiners who are appointed by the test centre and approved by British Council or IDP: IELTS Australia.

On pages 63–75 you will find candidates' answers to five sample Writing tests. There is one answer for each Writing task. Each answer has been awarded a Band Score and is accompanied by an examiner comment on the candidate's performance for that task.

The examiners' guidelines for assessing the Writing scripts are very detailed. There are many different ways a candidate may achieve a particular Band Score. The candidates' answers that follow should not be regarded as definitive examples of any particular Band Score.

Please refer to the public band descriptors for Writing on the IELTS website www.ielts.org

Academic Writing Example 1 – Task 1

Sample Script 1

The Japanese Tourists started travelling to Australia in 1985 were around 4.5 millions and in the following year it had gone up ¼ million more than 1985. The number of tourist increased steadily till 1990 from ½ million to 1½ millions and at the same time it there was, fell in the figure in 1991 about ¼ million tourists comparing the 1990 as one can say it surges. In 1992 it picked up again and gone upto 11 ¾ million tourists (ie) ¾ million more than the year 1991. In 1993 it reached up 12 million tourists and in 1994 and gone steadily increased till 1995. In 1994 it reached 13 ¾ million and in 1995 it touched around 15 ½ million tourists.

In the same time if you talk in percentage of the Japanese tourist between 1985 to 1995 (ie) Australia's share of Japan's tourist Market it stored from a percentage to 6 percentage in 1995 and at the same time it reached its peak in 1994 more than 6.25%. When you see the graph it gone upto 4.9% in 1989 and there was a surge again in 1990, and it was about 4.25%. The increased started from 1991 till 1994 at the rate of 2% approximately, every year and at last in 1995 the percentage dropped about .25%.

The highest Japanese tourists travelling abroad was in 1995 and at the same time highest percentage was 1994 (ie) 6.25%

Examiner comment

Band 5

This answer includes the main points of the information but these are inaccurately reported and hard to identify because so much detail is given. The figures are confused and sometimes inaccurate. The candidate has tried to organise the information logically, but linking is repetitive and not always clear. The range of vocabulary is enough to describe the information, and spelling is quite well controlled. The writer tries to use a wider range at times but makes errors in word choice and word formation. Similarly, the writer tries to use some complex sentences, but errors in grammar, especially in verb phrases, are common and make the writing difficult to understand in places. This is a good example of a Band 5 response.

Academic Writing Example 1 – Task 2

Sample Script 2

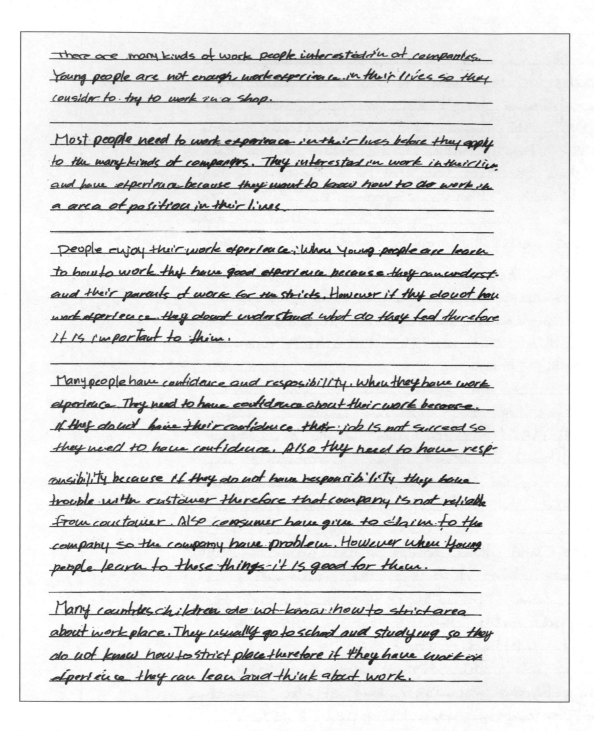

There are many kinds of work people interested in at companies. Young people are not enough work experience in their lives so they consider to try to work in a shop.

Most people need to work experience in their lives before they apply to the many kinds of companys. They interested in work in their lives and have experience because they want to know how to do work in a area of position in their lives.

People enjoy their work experience. When young people are learn to how to work they have good experience because they can understand and their parents of work for the stricts. However if they do not have work experience they dont understand what do they feel therefore it is important to them.

Many people have confidence and responsibility. When they have work experience. They need to have confidence about their work because. If they do not have their confidence their job is not succeed so they need to have confidence. Also they need to have responsibility because if they do not have responsibility they have trouble with customer therefore that company is not reliable from consumer. Also consumer have give to claim to the company so the company have problem. However when young people learn to those things it is good for them.

Many countries children do not know how to strict area about work place. They usually go to school and studying so they do not know how to strict place therefore if they have work experience they can learn and think about work.

Examiner comment

Band 3.5

This answer is obviously related to the topic, but there is no clear response to any part of the question and it is difficult to identify any relevant point of view. There is some attempt to use paragraphs and basic connectives, but there is little logical progression. Instead the ideas are very repetitive and circular both within and between paragraphs. The range of vocabulary is limited and so there is frequent repetition of basic vocabulary and words taken from the question. There are occasional examples of a wider range but there are also errors in word choice and spelling that confuse the reader. The candidate attempts to use a range of structures, but the lack of control of grammar and punctuation results in strain for the reader. Although the writing has some features of Band 4 performance, no part of the question is successfully addressed and this limits the rating to Band 3.5.

Academic Writing Example 2 – Task 1

> Different climate conditions need different structure of the house. The diagrams show us some principles of building a comfortable house for cool and for warm climats.
>
> We can see a house design which fits to the cool climate. Its building material is the heat storage and it has a high-angled roof which is flat and leaning in order to get more sunlight. The whole house which is built by the thermal building material is almost surrounded by the insulation. These two kind of building materials are used to avoid the loss of heat. Window is a very important part of the house. If the house is located in
>
> the place of the cool climate. Its window must be easy to recieve more sunlight, just like the one on the first diagram. It can be lighted directly by the sun.
>
> The second group of diagrams show the principles of house design for warm climate. Different from the first diagram, the house roof is not flat but angled. Because of the warm climate, the insulation is only built on the roof of the house, but its use has been changed. The material of the house roof is composed of insulation and the reflective roof material to keep the room from being influenced by the outside high temperature. The windows hide under the shade of the roof to prevent the sunlight from coming in. And windows are often closed in daytime and open in the night in order to make the heat go out with the circulation of air.

Examiner comment

Band 7

The answer focuses on the most significant information in the set of diagrams and effectively highlights the main differences between the two house designs. The opening paragraph could have provided a better introduction but, overall, ideas are arranged logically and the answer is well organised with clear linking and paragraphing. A good range of vocabulary and sentence structures is used, although there are some errors and the wording from the task is not paraphrased sufficiently. There is a range of sentence types and a good level of accuracy, even in complex sentences. Errors do not affect communication. Overall this is a clear example of a Band 7 response.

Academic Writing Example 2 – Task 2

Sample Script 4

Old buildings not only are still useful, but also keep the history alive. Not all of them have enough history to say that it's better to maintain it. In my opinion only the buildings that really involve nation's history could be maintain, because it will remain to the people the tradition, culture, and stories that relevant people lived before, and this is part of the formal education of each person.

Most of the countries of the world at least have important people that help to constructed the nation, or fight for the independence, or are just important because they changed the social, political, economical or even musical environment of their countries. When people see the places where their people lived and where they develop their arts, these places or buildings help to reconstruct the stories and are useful for imagine how was the situation before. So every time that people will see this buildings or monuments they are able to remain the history and also learn about it. Finally nowadays human beings are capable to maintain this buildings in good conditions, even they can modernize them but without change their principal structure and fronts.

On the other hand it's true that the cities of the world have to continue with its development. Therefore they have to build new buildings that allow people work with better and modern environments that let them work efficiently, and also that offer development resources. New buildings brings new technologie as well, that could improve the efficience, productivity and production of different companies, organizations, shops, offices, etc.

In conclussion some buildings would be knocked down to make way progress and development. However that old buildings that have important history for human beings should be maintain. If we knocked down these buildings we would knocked down our traditions, culture, history and even some part of our lives.

Examiner comment

Band 6

The answer addresses both questions in the task, but the second question is only treated in a general way and so this aspect is not sufficiently developed. Nevertheless there is a clear argument that progresses logically in spite of some repetition. Connectives are used but linking between sentences is sometimes omitted, while referencing is not always clear. The range of language is adequate for the task, and there are examples of some less common words, which are used appropriately. The candidate makes mistakes in word form and spelling, but the meaning is still clear. There is a range of structures, though complex structures are not always successful and errors in grammar and tense are noticeable. However, these do not usually cause problems for the reader. Overall this is a clear example of a Band 6 response.

Academic Writing Example 3 – Task 1

Sample Script 5

When we see the graph, domestic household is different of others. According to the graph number of complaints remained stable about factories noise from 1984 to 1966. It means most of skills and something are made from factories. However society is getting change, so in the future people don't have to go factories, they can do most of things' at home. May be factories will be decrease. Number of complaints dropped steadly about road works from 1980 to 1996. It shows us most of road works were formed in the past. Now days people don't have to road works because there already were todays. Number of complaints increased sharply about traffic noise from 1990 to 1996. It remained the same from 1980 to 1984 then it dropped from 1985 to 1988. However it increased from 1988, it means many people have their own car and society is getting change. Now-days cars are neccessary in our life and it will be increase continues.

Number of complaints reached almost peak about domestic household in 1996. It increased suddenly from 1990, and it is highest to others. It means people want domestic and many people did that.

Examiner comment

Band 4

There is no introduction to the topic in this answer, so the opening is rather confusing. The candidate has tried to describe the key information but gives no figures and the focus is lost in the irrelevant explanations and excessive detail. The information is not well selected or logically organised, so it is difficult to follow the message. New points are not linked into the summary and relationships between points are not clearly signalled, although some basic linking words are used. The range of vocabulary is limited and even though the writer tries to use a range of structures, there is a lack of grammatical control and frequent errors in quite basic structures.
This is a good example of a Band 4 response.

Academic Writing Example 3 – Task 2

Sample Script 6

The evolution in technology nowadays is very rampant. People do not even recognize changes from one to another. There are a lot of modern equipment, appliances and even simple machines are available in the market. Competitors in business industries keep doing transformation, product development and more research work. Sometimes their own products competi each other. One of these modern equipments or appliances in the market that is very salable is the television.

Television dominates the communication and entertainment industries long time ago. Starting from the Black and White TV, here comes the Colored TV. In addition, cable TV is now available in the market. In Southeast Asia, particularly in the Philippines, the most salable appliances in the market is the television. Even the ordinary vendors in the market or in the sidewalk avail one so that they can watch television while working. Business men and employees watch TV for news and general information. Housekeepers and house-wives, together with the children entertain themselves with the variety shows and soap operas through television. Everyone, in all walks of life uses television as one of their 'mate' in life. There are some issues that modernization, new technology including television is dangerous for children & for the whole family because it destroys a sense of community and belongingness and sometimes it influence the young people in their principle in life.

In conclusion, television is a modern appliance that can help a lot in the life of each and everyone. It has it's own disadvantages too. It can do good or can influence bad paradigms to the people, but I believe that the result of the use or watching TV depends on the person or family themselves. Together w/ the development is the consequence of having great discipline in oneself.

Examiner comment

Band 5

This answer does not focus sufficiently on the question and a lot of irrelevant material is included. It is difficult to identify the candidate's position on the topic or to extract the main ideas. There is some organisation, but the development of the answer is not wholly logical. A range of linking words is used, but these are sometimes inaccurate and in some sections the candidate does not clearly signal how ideas relate to each other. There is a clear attempt to use an ambitious range of vocabulary, but there are a lot of inappropriate choices that indicate limited control. Similarly, the writer uses a mix of complex and simple sentences but makes fairly basic errors. Although there are some features of higher level performance in this script, the lack of focus and clear development limit the overall rating to Band 5.

General Training Writing Example 1 – Task 1

Sample Script 7

Dear Sir or Madam

I'm writing with in joining the membership of your sports club.

I'm a new student of the college which is about 500 metres away from your sports club. There are no sports facilities in the college, but I'm interested in sports. From very young. I liked sport activities very well. I like swimming football, basket ball etc. Especially football. I played it everyday when I was in middle school. I'm a good middle field kicker in our

middle school football team.

I graduated from middle school this year and entered the college in this September. It's a pity that there are no sports field for football in the college. I was told many students of the college joined in your sports club to play football. I'd want know how I can join your sports club. Can you tell me how much membership fees for one year? Is there any additional condition to join your club?

Your early reply would be appreciated

Yours sincerely.

Examiner comment

Band 6

This letter has a clear purpose and the main points are covered clearly and adequately. There is some irrelevant supporting information, but the letter is generally appropriate in tone and content. The organisation of the letter is logical, and there is some good use of linking devices, although there are also errors and inappropriacies in this area. The range of vocabulary is sufficient for the task and there are some good expressions used appropriately in quite complex structures. However, sentences are sometimes incomplete, as in the opening sentence, and there are errors in grammar and punctuation. These do not generally cause problems for the reader. This is a clear example of a Band 6 response.

General Training Writing Example 1 – Task 2

Sample Script 8

Nowadays in many countries, the natives do not wear their national costumes. Most people prefer wearing dresses which are made in their country but not considered their traditional dresses. Some people do not approve of this by saying that this way, people are forgetting their history and traditions. But I think that it is a part of mordenization and development. We should look ahead and not backwards.

Almost every country has its traditional costumes and national dresses. Some are comfortable and some are difficult to handle. By comfortable I mean a dress being comfortable enough to be worn daily for your routine work. If we take the example of Pakistan's traditional dress Shalwar-Kameez, one can see that although it is a very comfortable night suit, wearing it for your office work, travelling on a motorbike, or a labourer working on a construction site, it gets quite uncomfortable and dangerous. Because of its design, shalwar kameez can obstruct various errands like cycling, hiking and especially after travelling, the dress becomes quite messed up and untidy. If you compare this to regular pants and a T-shirt, I believe they are the best piece of clothing to be worn for many different purposes.

Besides, for a developing nation or for a nation making progress in various fields of science and technology, garments are and should be a secondary thing. What good is history and tradition when a nation cannot make advancements in science and technology. What good is history when your living generation is dying of hunger and diseases. We should look toward economic, medical and social progress and not worry about small things like clothing and traditions.

Another aspect of development is the evolution. Traditional clothes were made centuries ago according to the requirement of that age. With the new computer age, the dress requirements have changed and old traditional clothes are no more ~~it~~ useful

Working towards one nation and one world, I believe the racial discrimination should finish now and we all should be one. We should not have segregation even through clothing because that leads to wars and hatred. The world in one and now the people should be one.

Examiner comment

Band 7.5

The answer is well-developed and well-focused. Overall there is a very good level of coherence and some quite sophisticated cohesive structures are used well. However, the final two paragraphs are less well-linked than the rest and there are occasional problems in referencing. Some very appropriate vocabulary and idiomatic usage is evident including repetition for clarity and effect. There are occasional minor inappropriacies and spelling slips but these do not affect understanding. A very good range of structures is used with confidence and accuracy. There are some lapses in control of grammar and punctuation, but these do not reduce clarity. Although the writing has many Band 8 features, the flaws in cohesion limit the rating to Band 7.5.

General Training Writing Example 2 – Task 1

Sample Script 9

Dear Sir or Madam

I feel I must express my disappointment
. I have received a new air conditioning system which has heating system
as well. It is a new design in this year,   convenient button
function, and   can fix on the wall. When I received, I was
absolutely delighted. However I was using for 3 nights. Unfortunately
I found some problems with it. Firstly If I switch it on it
was such a big noisy. Secondly, as we all know nowadays very
cold. Thus I bought this incredibly heating system doesn't working.
If I turn on the heating switch   only blew the cold wind.

Consequently I couldn't sleep over very well.

In addition, I had ordered marvelous violet colour. However
I received fair beige colour. it was quite unbalance with
my furnitures. I am still very upsetting.   I think that
is not reasonable cost. I paid over £ 2000.
I think you would consider to give me discount it if I
go to your shop again. And   Changing the another air conditiong
system and heating system which is violet colour as soon as possible.
I look forward to hearing from you shortly

Yours faithfully

Examiner comment

Band 5.5

This answer generally provides all the information required by the task, but the purpose seems incomplete without reference to the shop at the start of the letter. There is no reference to this being an item bought at the shop, even though it is evident that the writer is complaining. The answer is organised and there is a clear progression in the letter. The writing contains a range of connectives and some of these are used effectively to relate ideas. In some sections, however, these cohesive devices are used mechanically at the start of almost every sentence. The range of vocabulary is sufficient for the task and is a strong feature of the answer, in spite of some inappropriate word choice and some errors in word form. There is also a range of structures, with a mix of simple and complex sentences. However, control of syntax, basic grammar and punctuation is weak at times and errors are quite frequent. The flaws in setting out the purpose of the letter and the frequent grammatical error limit this script to Band 5.5.

General Training Writing Example 2 – Task 2

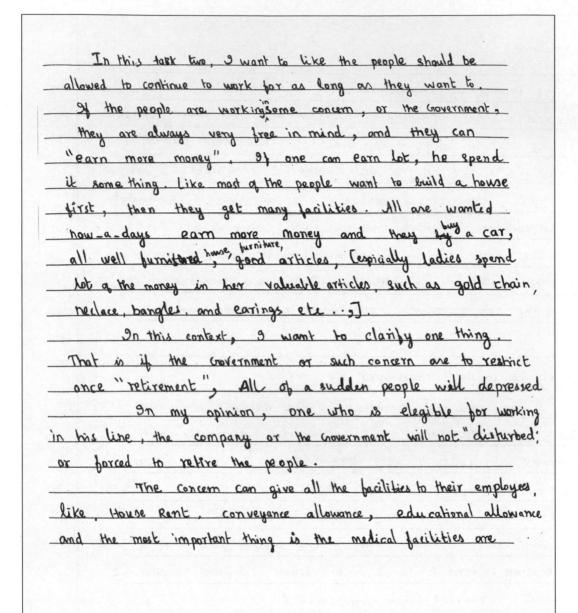

In this task two, I want to like the people should be allowed to continue to work for as long as they want to.

If the people are working in some concern, or the Government, they are always very free in mind, and they can "earn more money". If one can earn lot, he spend it some thing. Like most of the people want to build a house first, then they get many facilities. All are wanted now-a-days earn more money and they buy a car, all well furnished house, furniture, good articles, (espically ladies spend lot of the money in her valuable articles, such as gold chain, neclace, bangles, and earings etc..;]

In this context, I want to clarify one thing. That is if the Government or such concern are to restrict once "retirement", All of a sudden people will depressed

In my opinion, one who is elegible for working in his line, the company or the Government will not "disturbed" or forced to retire the people.

The concern can give all the facilities to their employees, like, House Rent, conveyance allowance, educational allowance and the most important thing is the medical facilities are provide for their employers. one who satisfied in his or her job, they can wonderfully worked for (his or her) concern. So the Government or any other companies are always give much more importants to the employers.

In my opinion again I will tell the companies & Governments "do not forced to retire at a particular age such as 60 or 65". In a person who is not able able to work in his 50th year, then he applied voluntary retirement. In this aspect the concern to must provide all the benefit to this person. Such as, provident fund, ESI, Merical allowance and retirement-benefits.

One who is satisfied his job, his life is automatically pleasent and his mind is peacefull. So the major companies are give more and more facilities.

Finally, I would like to request all the concerns, do not forced to ritire at a particular age limit in his employers. Please allowed people should enjoy and continue to work for as long as they want. This is in my view point, to tell the good companies and all the Governments.

Thanking you.

Examiner comment

Band 4.5

The answer focuses on the question, but is quite repetitive. Ideas are not well developed and lack clarity, and some supporting ideas seem to be irrelevant. It is difficult to follow the argument or to understand how ideas relate to each other. Linking expressions and paragraphing are used, but not appropriately, and this creates problems for the reader. The range of vocabulary is the best feature of this answer as it is sufficient for a discussion of the topic, in spite of repetition of some inappropriate word choices. The control of grammar and sentence structures is weak, however, and the number of errors makes it difficult for the reader to extract the meaning at times. The range of vocabulary raises this script to Band 4.5.

How Speaking is assessed:
Sample Candidate Speaking Tests and Examiner Comment

The Speaking test assesses whether candidates can communicate effectively in English. Ratings are awarded on the basis of the features of performance displayed by a candidate across the test.

Candidate performance is rated using detailed performance descriptors. These describe spoken performance at the nine IELTS bands and are confidential.

Speaking is assessed according to four different criteria:

Fluency and Coherence
This criterion refers to the ability to talk with normal levels of continuity, rate and effort and to link ideas and language together to form coherent, connected speech. The key indicators of fluency are speech rate and speech continuity. The key indicators of coherence are logical sequencing of spoken sentences, clear marking of stages in a discussion, narration or argument, and the use of cohesive devices (e.g. connectors, pronouns and conjunctions) within and between sentences.

Lexical Resource
This criterion refers to the range of vocabulary the candidate can use and the precision with which meanings and attitudes can be expressed. The key indicators are the variety of words used, the adequacy and appropriacy of the words used, and the ability to paraphrase or circumlocute (get round a vocabulary gap by using other words) with or without noticeable hesitation.

Grammatical Range and Accuracy
This criterion refers to the range and the accurate and appropriate use of the candidate's grammatical resource. The key indicators of grammatical range are the length and complexity of the spoken sentences, the appropriate use of subordinate clauses, and the range of structures and sentence forms. The key indicators of grammatical accuracy are the frequency of grammatical errors in a given performance and the communicative effect of such errors.

Pronunciation
This criterion refers to the ability to produce comprehensible speech to fulfil the Speaking test requirements. The key indicators are the range of phonological features used to convey meaning, the amount of strain caused to the listener, and the amount of the speech which is unintelligible.

All criteria have equal weighting. The final Speaking score is reported as a whole band or a half band.

Speaking performances are assessed by certificated examiners who are appointed by the test centre and approved by British Council or IDP: IELTS Australia.

On the CD you will find three candidate Speaking tests. On page 77 you will find the examiner comments on each test and the bands awarded.

The examiners' guidelines for assessing the Speaking performance of candidates are very detailed. There are many different ways a candidate may achieve a particular Band Score. The candidates' performances on the CD should not be regarded as definitive examples of any particular Band Score.

Please refer to the public band descriptors for Speaking on the IELTS website www.ielts.org

Speaking test Example 1: Pakistani male

Band 7.5

The candidate speaks rapidly but fluently and his responses are relevant and well developed. He uses a sophisticated range of markers and cohesive devices. There is some repetition, but this has no effect on coherence. He uses a wide range of vocabulary with confidence and ease. There are many examples of precise idiomatic usage and good collocation. Inaccuracies are rare and minor. Overall, his control of grammar is a little weaker than other features of his performance. Though many sentences are correct, and he uses a wide range of sentence types, there are article and preposition problems and some verb form errors. These limit the rating for this criterion. He can be followed throughout the test, and he uses intonation and stress to good communicative effect. There are many examples of very natural speech. However, the speed of his speech, coupled with his strong accent, results in the marked pronunciation of some words. This is a high-level candidate whose variable grammatical control limits his rating to Band 7.5.

Speaking test Example 2: Thai female

Band 5

The candidate keeps going but she relies on strategies such as repetition and listing, and she has a slightly slow delivery. Some cohesive devices are used but she often resorts to 'yes' when she cannot complete an idea. Her sentences become disjointed at times and she loses fluency as her language becomes more complex. She manages to respond in all sections of the test and produces some adequate vocabulary. However, her limitations are apparent in her use of simple expressions, such as 'very nice' and 'something like that', and there is a lot of repetition. Despite attempts to use complex language, most of her sentences are simple. Some are incomplete and many contain errors. She uses mainly present tenses with noticeable omissions of articles and prepositions. There is occasional mispronunciation of words, such as 'clothes' and 'grammar', caused by her confusion/ omission of individual sounds. Overall, however, she can be understood and she is beginning to use word stress and intonation to express her ideas. This candidate achieves
a range of marks that result in an overall Band 5.

Speaking test Example 3: Iranian female

Band 6.5

The candidate gives long responses but she hesitates at times and repeatedly uses 'erm', which limits her fluency. She links her ideas using a range of connectives and markers but she uses some inaccurately. Her range of vocabulary is a strong feature of her interview, although her performance dips slightly in Part 2. She can use less common vocabulary, collocations and idiomatic expressions to good effect. However, there are examples of error and inappropriate word use. A range of sentence types is used and many of these are correct. She has good control of tenses and modal verbs. Conditionals are frequent and often accurate, and there are many examples of complex structures. However, there are some basic errors in preposition and pronoun use, as well as errors in word order. Her pronunciation is very clear but words are frequently over-pronounced and her speech is monotonous and jerky. Occasional confusion is caused by mispronunciation of words. The candidate has a strong lexical and structural base, but there is an effort involved in the way she speaks. This limits her rating to Band 6.5.

Completing the Answer Sheets

Candidates are required to transfer their answers to an Answer Sheet for the Listening, Academic Reading and General Training Reading tests. Ten minutes extra time is allowed for transferring answers at the end of the Listening but not for the Reading. The Answer Sheet is double-sided; candidates write their Listening answers on one side and then turn over and write their Reading answers on the other side. After marking at the test centre, all Answer Sheets are returned to Cambridge ESOL for analysis.

An example of a completed Listening Answer Sheet is given below for guidance. It is important that candidates complete their personal details at the top of the Answer Sheet and follow the instructions for transfer of answers. Please note the advice given for completion of the Answer Sheet.

Candidates must take care when writing their answers on the Answer Sheet, as poor spelling and grammar are penalised.

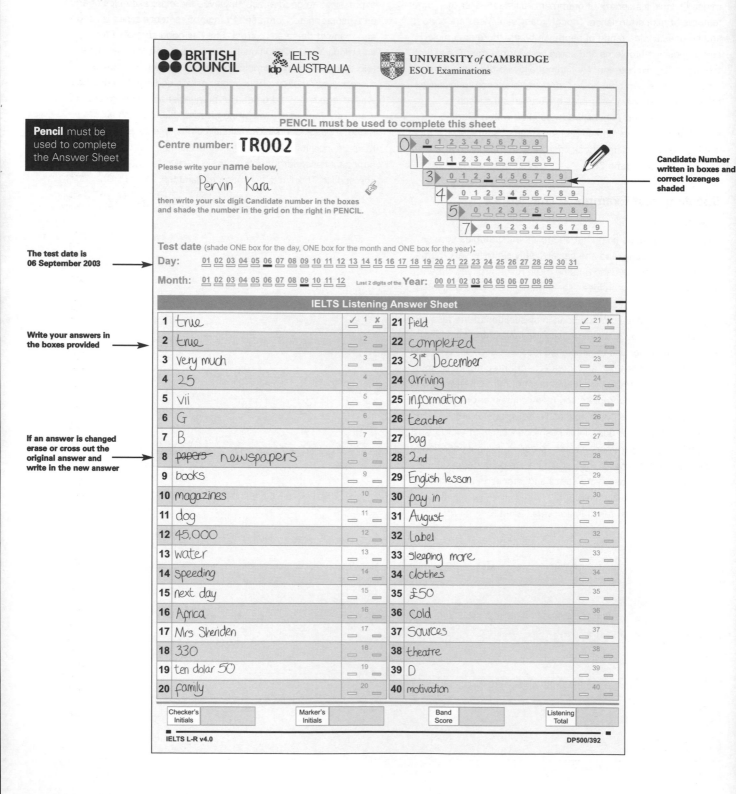

Pencil must be used to complete the Answer Sheet

The test date is 06 September 2003

Write your answers in the boxes provided

If an answer is changed erase or cross out the original answer and write in the new answer

Candidate Number written in boxes and correct lozenges shaded

IELTS Listening Answer Sheet

1	true	21	field
2	true	22	completed
3	very much	23	31st December
4	25	24	arriving
5	vii	25	information
6	G	26	teacher
7	B	27	bag
8	papers newspapers	28	2nd
9	books	29	English lesson
10	magazines	30	pay in
11	dog	31	August
12	45,000	32	label
13	water	33	sleeping more
14	speeding	34	clothes
15	next day	35	£50
16	Africa	36	cold
17	Mrs Sheriden	37	sources
18	330	38	theatre
19	ten dolar 50	39	D
20	family	40	motivation

Listening Answer Sheet

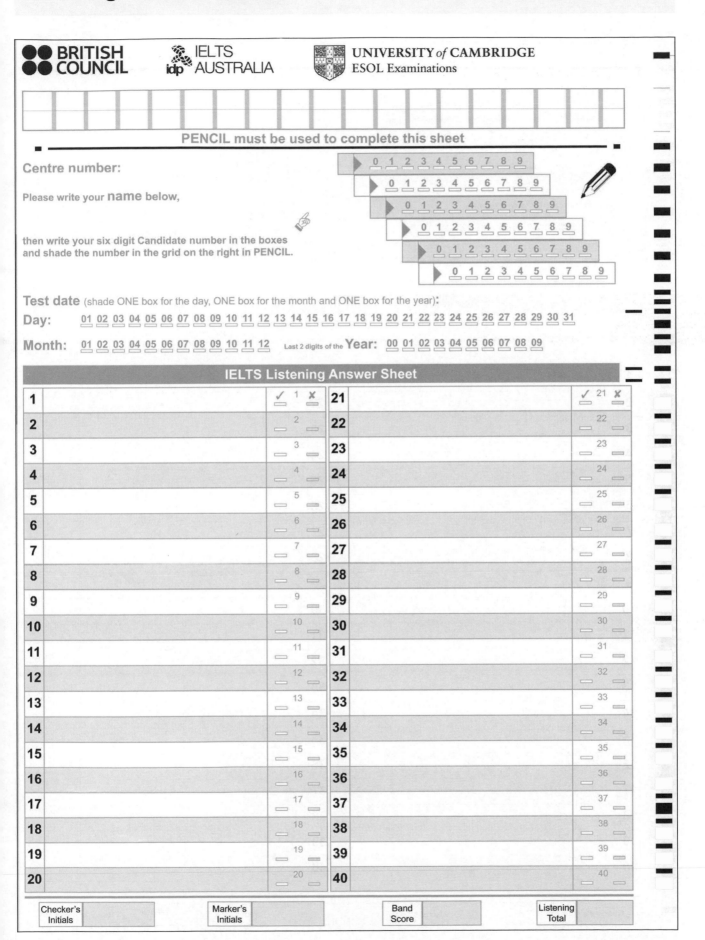

Reading (Academic and General Training) Answer Sheet

Are you: Female? ▭   Male? ▭

Your first language code:
▶ 0 1 2 3 4 5 6 7 8 9
▶ 0 1 2 3 4 5 6 7 8 9
▶ 0 1 2 3 4 5 6 7 8 9

IELTS Reading Answer Sheet

Module taken (shade one box):   Academic ▭   General Training ▭

#		✓ ✗	#		✓ ✗
1		1	21		21
2		2	22		22
3		3	23		23
4		4	24		24
5		5	25		25
6		6	26		26
7		7	27		27
8		8	28		28
9		9	29		29
10		10	30		30
11		11	31		31
12		12	32		32
13		13	33		33
14		14	34		34
15		15	35		35
16		16	36		36
17		17	37		37
18		18	38		38
19		19	39		39
20		20	40		40

Checker's Initials		Marker's Initials		Band Score		Reading Total	

Writing (Academic and General Training) Answer Sheet

WRITING ANSWER SHEET

Candidate Name: .... Candidate Number: ....

Centre Name: .... Date: ....

Module: ACADEMIC ☐   GENERAL TRAINING ☐   (Tick as appropriate)

TASK 1

_____

_____

_____

_____

_____

_____

_____

_____

_____

_____

_____

_____

| EXAMINER'S USE ONLY |

EXAMINER 2 NUMBER: ....

CANDIDATE NUMBER: ....   EXAMINER 1 NUMBER: ....

_____

_____

_____

_____

_____

_____

_____

_____

_____

_____

_____

_____

_____

_____

_____

_____

_____

_____

_____

_____

_____

_____

_____

EXAMINER'S USE ONLY

EXAMINER 2 TASK 1

TA		CC		LR		GRA	

UNDERLENGTH		NO OF WORDS		PENALTY	
OFF-TOPIC		MEMORISED		ILLEGIBLE	

EXAMINER 1 TASK 1

TA		CC		LR		GRA	

UNDERLENGTH		NO OF WORDS		PENALTY	
OFF-TOPIC		MEMORISED		ILLEGIBLE	